COTTAGE ON THE GREEN

ROWLAND PARKER

WITH LINE DRAWINGS BY THE AUTHOR

LONDON
THE RESEARCH PUBLISHING COMPANY
52 LINCOLN'S INN FIELDS

ISBN 0 7050 0019 2

Made and printed in Gt. Britain for The Research Publishing Co.
(Fudge & Co. Ltd), London, by Biddles Ltd, Guildford, Surrey

CONTENTS

PROLOGUE

I had been living in the cottage for about seventeen years before I ever gave more than a passing thought to its history, or even considered that it had one. For me it was, first and last, a home, somewhere to live. I knew that it was pretty old, and I cursed its antiquity every time I had to patch a crumbling wall or remove a shovelful of brown dust which had once been part of an oak beam. I considered it rather quaint, and at certain times, especially after the periodical re-painting, or when the hollyhocks and roses half hid the front door, I found it very picturesque. I still do. Occasional visitors referred to it as "a gem". But it was still just a house. A very small house. Small houses do not have a "history". They have always belonged to unimportant people like me, who do not figure in history.

Then, one day in 1962, I had reason to transfer my account to another branch of the same bank. I remembered that there was a bundle of deeds and papers originally surrendered as security for a loan, and thought that it would be a good idea to verify that they had been transferred also. Never having seen the documents, and having repaid the loan long since, I asked out of sheer curiosity if I might see them. To my surprise, I was handed a parcel, wrapped in brown paper, big enough to fill a suit-case, and was told that these were "only the old deeds". The "ones which mattered" constituted yet another bundle. Highly intrigued, I took the parcel home, and amused myself for several evenings by looking casually through the headings and dates to see just how "old" they were. The earliest deed bore the date 1772, and for several months afterwards I derived a ridiculous satisfaction, and an inane sense of superiority, from being able to disclose in a seemingly casual manner to my friends and acquaintances, especially to any who happened to live in a brand-new house, that "the deeds of my property date back nearly two hundred years."

The house remained very much in the forefront of my mind. But it was with the present rather than the past that I was concerned. The thatch had recently been renewed, so I felt secure on that point for the time being. Something, however, had to be done about the floors, which were worn, uneven, impossible to keep clean, and too near the ceilings. A new kitchen had to be built, even if it meant pulling down half the cottage; which it didn't, fortunately, and thanks to the consideration which the architect showed for the original fabric. Had his plans been followed to the letter, not a single bit of the original fabric would have suffered. But in the event the builder was faced with an impossible task, and was obliged to tear out the lower half of the gable-end on to which the kitchen was being built. A few hefty hammer-blows brought down the infilling of "wattle and daub" with its plaster coating; the beams or "studs" were wrenched away by hand after a vain attempt to saw off the worm-eaten lower ends. Several million ants beat a hasty retreat, fighting as they went, some of them finding refuge in the workmen's trousers.

It was whilst engaged in sawing those discarded beams into logs that I began to reflect. There is ample time for reflection when you are sawing through oak beams six inches and more in thickness. Just how old were those chunks of wood? An oak-tree grows for two or three hundred years before it is ripe for felling, maybe much longer in an era when oak-trees are more plentiful, in an area far from ship-building yards. Maybe four or five hundred years. Once seasoned and shaped, the wood, if kept dry and not too badly attacked by woodworm, was almost indestructible except by fire. It could be used over and over again, transferred from one building to another, from one century to another. The beams which I was then in the act of destroying could have been beams for five or six hundred years. They could have been shaped by somebody at about the time when Columbus was accidentally re-discovering America! The tree from which they were cut could have been planted by somebody — or some bird or squirrel — at about the time when King William's commissioners were compiling the Domesday survey! There was I obliterating a small, though very tough particle of history. I finished the sawing, and the logs were soon consumed in the ensuing winter days, but the reflections continued, took on a more definite shape, and eventually crystallised into a firm resolve to explore the history of the cottage.

CHAPTER I
Search

It seemed a straightforward task. There was the cottage. There were the documents. I spent a few days giving the cottage what I thought was a thorough inspection, made a few notes and sketches, then tackled the documents. I soon became absorbed in the story which slowly emerged from amidst the many thousands of words. The handwriting in itself was quite a fascination, though it soon became evident that precise locations and definitions were not to be expected. The various bits of land concerned were "lying dispersed in the common fields of Foxton". The house was "one messuage or tenement, with barn, croft of pasture, and their appurtenances in Foxton". Any description usually ended with the qualification "or howsoever otherwise or in whatsoever other manner or by whatsoever other name or names quantities or descriptions the said tenements now are or at any time heretofore have been bounded or described." If the voice of the Law could be as vague as that, who was I to be so fussy? I had been quite busy and happy for several weeks when I came to a real puzzle. The cottage whose history I had so far traced over a period of 80 years or so was quite definitely not this cottage, but one situated in Stocker's Lane (now Station Road) half a mile from here. I suddenly remembered my compulsory purchase of six other cottages when I had bought this. Odd that I should have forgotten it, but I had. I had been tracing the history of one of those six. The deeds were still in my possession because they no longer "mattered". I wonder how many other people are in possession of deeds to which they are not entitled? My sense of guilt was quickly replaced by one of dismay when I realised that I knew nothing whatever about the history of my cottage prior to 1830. It was quite hopeless to continue.

It was quite impossible not to continue. I was too deeply involved by now. The word "straightforward" was really to blame for my foolish mistake. Of course one does not work forward, nor does one work straight. One works backward, from the known into the unknown. What did I know of the history of the cottage? I knew all its history from 1830 to the present day. I had in my possession – lawfully – an extract from the Enclosure Award of 1830, the first document ever to give a detailed description and location of every bit of property in the parish. Moreover, it was accompanied by a map, of which I had obtained a photo-copy (thanks to the services of the County Record Office at the Shire Hall) and the text was clarified by reference to numbers on the map. The description of my estate begins: "All that garden orchard and homestead *called Docwra's* - - "

Who was Docwra? Did he live here? Did he own the cottage? In 1830 the cottage had been "owned" by John Bendysh, Esq., Lord of the Manor of Foxton Bury with Wimbish and Chatteris; it was copyhold of that manor. The books and rolls of the manor are, as they ought to be, in the County Record Office. I had only to search diligently – working backward! – through the books until I came to the name of Docwra. I spent one whole day and half of the next, in January 1966, plodding through hundreds of entries, each consisting of hundreds, in some cases thousands, of words. I stopped at 1733, prior to which date the entries are in Latin. My eyes and head could endure no more. There was never a trace of the name Docwra. There was no man called Docwra in Foxton. There never had been — as I later discovered. How, then, could the cottage be called Docwra's?

It was Mr. Farrar, the County Archivist, who first mentioned "Docwra's Manor", a house situated in Shepreth about a mile away. I had seen it many times, had even heard, and forgotten, its name, but I knew nothing about it. Neither did Mr. Farrar, and a quick reference to his catalogue suggested that the Archives could throw no light on the subject. But his library could. The obvious source of information on manorial history was "Lysons", i.e. the Cambridgeshire volume of a mighty work entitled "Magna Britannia", compiled by the Rev. D. Lysons and S. Lysons, published in 1808. Writing of Foxton, Lysons says:

> "this manor (De la Hayes) having been divided into moities, which passed by other marriages to the families of Dockwra and Wimbish, they were afterwards esteemed separate manors, being called after the names of their owners; having passed severally through various families, they have again been united, and are both the property of Mr. Bendysh."

Writing of Shepreth:

> "The manors of Dockwra's and Wimbish were formerly one, which was successively in the families of De la Haye and Engayne; having been divided into moities, between the Blitons and St. Georges, they became two manors, called, from subsequent proprietors, Dockwra's and Wimbish; they were again united by purchase in the family of Ingrey, and, by successive conveyances, passed to the Hancocks and Richardsons and, by bequest, to the Hales; having been a second time separated Dockwra's now belongs to Mr. Woodham — has been in Mr. Woodham's family since 1759 and, during the preceding century, had passed through the families of Ladkin, Plover, Hunt, Comber and Fairchild."

Where did all that get me? It taught me nothing about my cottage, or so I thought at the time. I had, however, learnt two more valuable lessons. One was that the tracing of manorial history is a very complicated business. Secondly — and this came as rather a shock, though later I learned to accept it as normal — that historical authorities can be unreliable, misleading and inaccurate. It was obvious that there were at least *two* manors of Docwra's. A history of the Docwra family might help. By pure chance — and chance was becoming my ally — Mr. W. G. Stevens of Newnham, with whom Mr. Farrar put me in contact, had written a short history of the family. This proved interesting and helpful in some respects, especially later, but seemed to bring me no nearer to my target. What I needed was the court-books of the manor or manors of Docwra's, — and they did not seem to exist.

After some weeks of intermittent reflection — bright ideas never come to one as quickly as one would like to suppose — it occurred to me to wonder: where did Lysons get his information from? He and his brother could not possibly have done all the detailed research necessary for the compilation of the histories of hundreds of manors. There must have been a source readily accessible to them.

There was. William Cole (1714-1782), one-time parson of Milton, later of Bletchley, spent some thirty years of his life visiting Cambridgeshire parishes, churches and manor-houses with a view to writing a county history. His work was never completed or published, but practically all his notes have survived in manuscript form, and are now in the British Museum. Microfilm copies of these MSS are in the County Record Office, with excellent facilities for viewing. I had already looked at some, without finding anything which seemed relevant to my purpose. I had evidently not used sufficient care, for when I came to look again at Additional MS No. 5823, pp 32-37, I found an account of the manors of Wimbish and Docwra, tantalisingly incomplete, but ending with this:

> "– it is now divided into 3 parts of which Toby Palavazine had the Royalty or Manor called Foxton Wimbish, and the demeans *one half to Philip Welbore,* Gent. – whose son John Welbore now enjoys the same. *The other half was sold to one Campion, whose Grandson, Samuel Campion of Foxton now holds it.*"

Practice was sharpening my wits. Cole wrote in the mid-18th century. Philip Welbore died in 1615. How, then, could Cole say "now" of something which happened a hundred years previously? Only by copying verbatim from somebody writing a hundred years previously.

This somebody, I soon discovered, was John Layer (1586-1640) who lived at Shepreth, became a Justice of the Peace, Lord of the Manor of Tyrell's, and spent much of his time travelling the district and writing notes on the villages and, more particularly, on the families which he considered "notable". He never reached the point of publication, but copied and re-copied his notes, often getting them mixed up in the process. Many of his manuscripts went astray, along with others which he had collected, sometimes by rather dubious means, for he was a veritable magpie where historical documents were concerned. Many were in their turn "collected" by Cole (who found one of them being used to wrap sugar in a grocer's shop in Royston) and incorporated in his own work. There are nine different sets of notes on the Cambs. villages. The late Dr. W. M. Palmer of Melbourn and Linton collated and edited extracts from them in his book "John Layer, Historian of Shepreth". In one of these MSS Layer, writing of Wimbish manor, says:

> "The manor is now divided into mean men's hands only – John Welbore, gent. sonne of Phillip, gent. hath the house, *one Campion a yeoman,* and Hancock the manor."

In another MS he writes:

> "Mortimer's is in mean men's hands only; John Welbore, gent. hath the house, one Campion a yeoman, and Hancock hath the manor."

Undeterred by Layer's obvious inability to distinguish between the manors of Mortimer's Wimbish and Docwra's, and stimulated if anything by his disdainful dismissal of those "mean" men, I was at last on the trail of somebody whose name I knew, and he was not called Docwra. Hancock could be ruled out, for Mr. Stevens had established that he was a Shepreth man, and had no connection with Foxton. My targets were Welbore and Campion. The Foxton Parish Registers provided me with lots of details. Transcripts of the Registers from 1599 to 1678, lodged in the University Library and kindly made available by Mrs. Owen, keeper of the Ely Diocesan Records, provided me with many more. Several visits to the University Archives brought to light copies of wills and inventories, made available by the courtesy of Miss Peak, the Archivist, and her assistant, Miss Raven.

I was getting somewhere at last, and I knew that I was on the right track. But I still had not found those books of the Manor of Docwra's. In January 1967 I wrote, not very hopefully, to the Historical Manuscripts Commission in Chancery Lane. To my amazement and delight, they sent an impressive list, with the information that some of the documents were in the County Record Office, the rest with a firm of Royston solicitors. The latter informed me, after a week of patient search, that their bundle had been handed over to the County Record Office some years previously.

So back to the Shire Hall once more. The missing books were found, and eagerly consulted. They began, in extract form, at 1504, and continued somewhat sporadically to the 19th century. They brought light on Ingrey, Hancock, Welbore, John Layer even. But not a word about Campion. As was so often the case, what seemed useless at the time was to prove of value later, but my immediate reaction was one of dismay at my failure to pin down this elusive Campion. To dismay was added bewilderment at the fact that, in these books of the Manor of Docwra's, the name of Docwra occurred *once* only, in 1565.

In desperation, I decided to take another look at the books of the Foxton Bury manor. To be precise, the Rolls of that manor-court, for from 1492 to the end of the 17th century they are in fact rolls of parchment – "membranes" is the technical term. They number hundreds; each is about four feet long and eighteen inches wide. Many are tattered and torn, some completely illegible in places where countless hands and sleeves have rubbed the surface; and, of course, all are written in Latin. I feared that the latter fact would prove an insuperable difficulty, until I discovered that the Latin of the 16th and 17th century clerks was little better than my own, once I had mastered a few technical terms and formulae. The real difficulty lay in deciphering the handwriting and the many abbreviations. Once again Mr. Farrar saved me from foundering, though I really had no right to impose upon him as I did. A County Archivist ought not to be expected to play the role of schoolmaster – but he did. And here, in the rolls from 1559 to 1612, where it had no business to be, was the whole history of the Campions! Campions in every other entry on every membrane. The explanation, simple but slow to dawn, is that the Campions had been first tenants of the Bury manor, then owners or part-owners of the Docwra manor.

As the field of knowledge extended, so my appetite increased. There was still a wide gap between 1680 and 1830. In March 1967, at the County Record Office, a careful search of the catalogue, now much more complete than it had been two years before, revealed the existence of a bundle of documents under the title "Woodham Bequest". From it I learnt a lot about the history of Shepreth, and of that part of the Docwra manor which was in Shepreth. Nothing of immediate relevance. Then it occurred to me that, since there was a Woodham Bequest by way of funeral oration to the Shepreth manors, there might be, there *ought* to be, a "Bendysh Bequest" fulfilling a similar office for the Foxton manors.

There was! ! ! The largest collection of documents I had yet seen! Nine bundles, weighing maybe half a hundredweight, not yet catalogued, but just as they were handed over by the Solicitors who had been the last Stewards of the

Manor of Foxton Bury with Wimbish and Chatteris, Mortimers and Docwra's. I had on numerous occasions cursed the legal fraternity for their habit of taking a thousand words to say what I could say in twenty, but now I was to bless them for it. These indentures and deeds described in great detail all the manors and told the story of their passage through the hands of Welbore, Seddon, Hatton and Parker to Bendysh. Heaven only knows what they must have cost! The final deed of sale covers nearly fifteen square yards of parchment and runs to over 12,000 words. The whole lot would have roofed my cottage easily! The mass of information included, of course, a detailed survey of the "Manor of Dockwrays or Dockways or Dockras, formerly in the tenure or occupation of John Moulton and *William Rayner* and now William Hurrell." I was on a straight course at last, and could see exactly where I was going.

The role of the Welbores was obviously paramount, and their wills were at Somerset House, along with all the wills proved in the Prerogative Court of Canterbury. The Principal Probate Registry "does not normally supply copies of wills more than a hundred years old", but, as these wills were readily accessible, a well-disposed official would be pleased to send copies of all four which I had requested (I was able to quote dates and catalogue numbers). These wills, dated 1615, 1661, 1675, and 1722, proved of immense value. The pieces of my jig-saw puzzle now amounted to hundreds. Yet I was to find as many more again – knowing by now exactly what I wanted – in further visits to the University Archives, the County Record Office and the University Library. Much of my spare time during the last three years has been spent in fitting the pieces together. There are still a few pieces missing, surprisingly few. When I embarked on this task, with about one eighth of the puzzle complete and just one other piece in my hand, I did not really believe that it could be done, that one could bring to light the continuous history of one small house over 500 years. What kept me going was the sheer challenge of the seemingly impossible. I commend it to anyone who is at a loss for something to occupy the mind. You may well say: "What a vain, useless way to spend one's time!" If that is how you feel, dear Sir or Madam, close the book now and read no further. If, on the other hand, you understand, perhaps even share the satisfaction which was mine – read on.

CHAPTER II
The Oak speaks

Many a time did I turn aside from the welter of words to look at those oak beams and think: "You could tell a rare story, you beams, if you could only speak." Few things are more stolidly mute than an oak beam. And yet, helped by that welter of words, one comes eventually to a stage at which one can read in the scarred face of those silent members something of the story which the structure of any old house inevitably enfolds.

The prime object of almost any archaeological exercise is to answer the question "How old is it?" Applied to a house, the question usually evokes more untruthful answers even than when applied to a woman, the untruth being in an opposite direction in each case. Scores of "XIVth century buildings" have been demolished or preserved in recent years, most of them dating from the sixteenth or seventeenth centuries. Actual dates inscribed on buildings are rare; and many are misleading, being an observance of fashion rather than fact. There is no date anywhere on this house. The representative of the Historic Monuments Commission, after a brief survey, placed it in Category II with the label "c. 1600". Anybody can see with half an eye that it qualifies for the vague classification of "Tudor cottage". But Tudor times extended from 1485 to 1603, and "Tudor" houses were still being built long after the latter date. Is there any scrap of archaeological evidence other than the fabric of the building?

There are in fact two; both brought to light, appropriately enough, by the spade. One does not normally do an archaeological dig in one's own house, but we had to. In the summer of 1958 we decided to replace the rough brick floor with one of concrete. Since the main reason for doing this was to enable me to walk about the living-room without banging my head on the too-too-solid beam which spanned the ceiling, it meant lowering the floor by eight inches in the middle. That meant excavating to a depth of eighteen inches in places. My wife and I removed all the bricks, and set aside those which were not already broken to be broken up and used as hard-core. Then we dug out, bucketful by bucketful, and removed, barrow-load after barrow-load, sixty-six loads in all, the layer of trodden clunch which had formed the original floor, and several inches of hard dry earth below it. What sustained us in this arduous labour – apart from the obvious fact that, once begun, the task had to be completed – was the firm conviction that we should unearth a buried treasure of some sort, or perhaps a skeleton, evidence of some long-hidden crime.

We did indeed find some bones, half a dozen sheep bones, yellow with age. I at once thought of some starving peasant stealing a sheep and burying the evidence, fatal evidence, of his crime. The true significance of the find only came to me about eight years later, when I read George Ewart Evans's "The Pattern Under the Plough", from which, by kind permission of the publishers (Faber and Faber), I quote:

" – when the wool merchant or farmer built his house he did not neglect to take the traditional steps to propitiate fortune and to avert evil from the spot where he hoped to spend the rest of his days. – The ways in which he did this are still to be found in these fifteenth and sixteenth-century houses, small and usually obscure

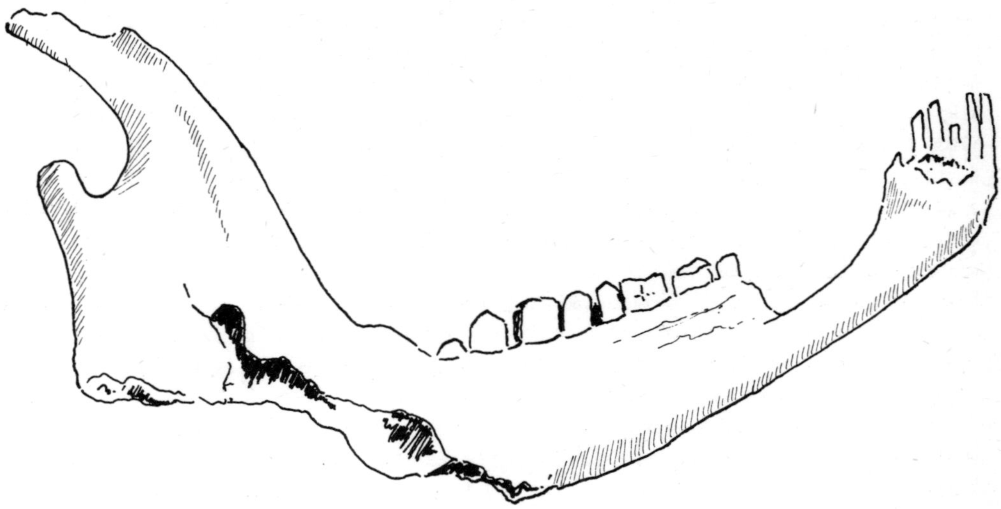

Fig. 1 To ensure that his house would stand as long as it deserved.

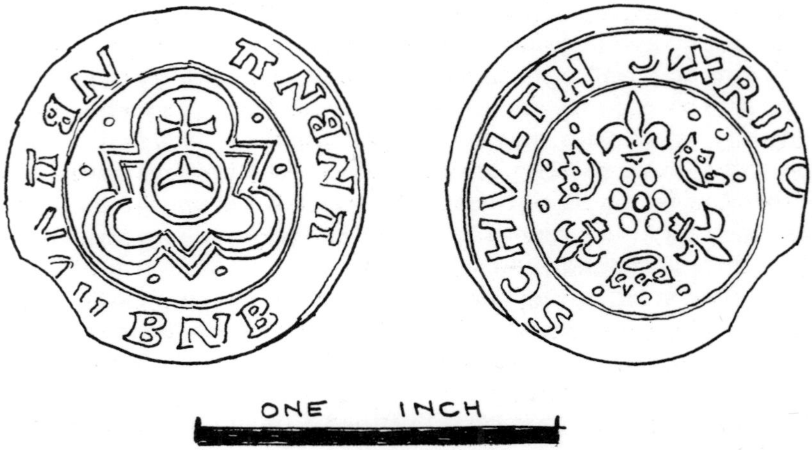

Fig. 2 Token.

evidences of a ceremony, implied or perhaps actually carried out by the owner or his surrogates the carpenters, to ensure that his house would stand as long as it deserved; and that its occupiers would prosper and escape the many misfortunes that had been too evident in their time; plague, sword, fire and all the evils that attend on a weak or unsettled government. A foundation sacrifice was the most ancient method – and the victim was buried in the 'footings'. Later it was considered sufficient for his shadow to be 'bricked in' to the foundations; and later still an animal became a substitute victim. By the late Middle Ages the bones of an animal were the usual apotropaic device, or just the animal's image carved on the building. Bones, either buried in the foundations, built into the flint wall or concealed in the wattle and daub or somewhere about the structure of the house, are commonly found in East Anglian houses."

The actual dating evidence thus provided is slight, though it may well point to a greater antiquity than was hitherto suspected.

The other scrap of archaeological evidence did suggest a date. When unearthed – from what depth I cannot say with any certainty, for we had neither the time nor the patience for careful excavation – I took it to be a halfpenny. It was later found to be a "token", crudely minted and much abraded, one of thousands which were minted in Nuremburg and used all over western Europe. It bears no date, but is known to have been issued between 1575 and 1585. These tokens were used in lieu of coins, representing usually a penny or halfpenny, at a time when small-value coinage was scarce. Originally of fine workmanship, they declined in quality towards the end of the sixteenth century. There are many to be found locally; I know of several identical with that which we found. Its main interest for me is that it indicates some building activity in the cottage around the year 1580.

Now as regards the timber. I will try to avoid too many technicalities, and refer generally to all pieces of timber as "beams", though I know that there are studs, trusses, purlins, rafters, joists, plates etc. There are 209 separate beams – separate in one sense, but every one joined to at least one other – not counting a few which I know to be recent insertions, and a dozen or so which I know to have been removed. The majority are in very sound condition, though some have been badly eroded by woodworm, and a few, especially those in actual contact with the earth, have rotted away to a rich brown powder. The first interesting feature about these beams is that 34 of them bear unmistakable signs of having been used before, in some other position or for some other purpose; some which are now vertical were once horizontal, and so on. This is particularly true of the main upright beams, six in all, one at each corner of the house and two in the centre. One might well suppose, from their size, that these six are the mainstay of the house, and were the first to be put into place. This is clearly not so, however, for the biggest of them had completely rotted away at the base, and was standing on nothing for a long time, yet that corner of the house did not sag or lean in the slightest. The truth is that the method of construction, crude though it may look, is very clever in that it distributes the weight over the whole frame, each member bearing only a small fraction of the total weight. My sketch shows something of this evidence of re-use, also the double wall-plate at the S.W. corner, where the

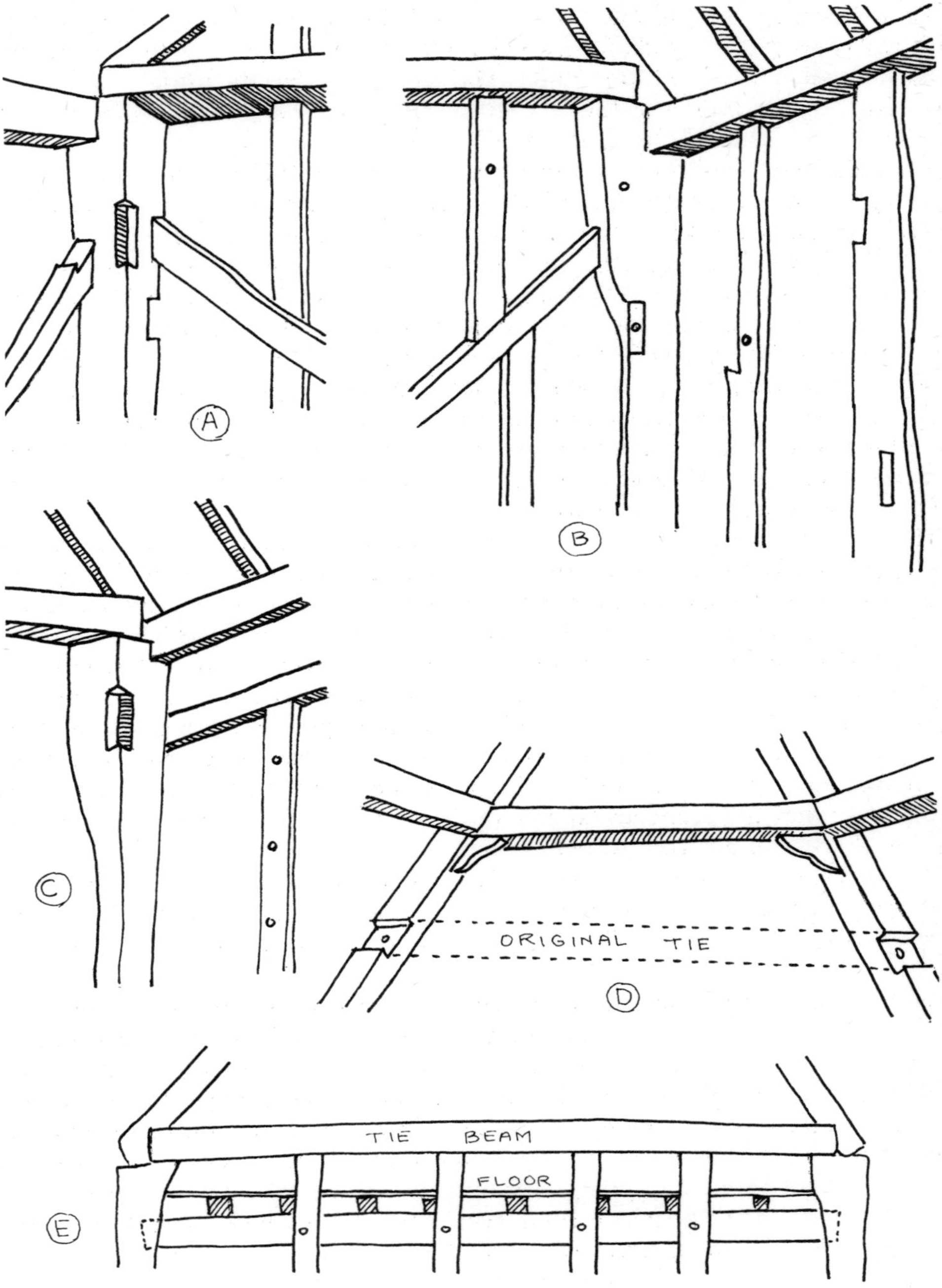

Fig. 3 *Sketches showing: A, B and C - - the re-use of timbers; D - - the raising of a roof-tie; E - - the insertion of the chamber floor.*

original plate now supports nothing.

Then there are the "foundations". It is difficult to imagine a house being built today without foundations. Yet for centuries people did so build their houses, small houses like this one. The only foundation, until well on into the 16th century, was the lower edge of the frame, a horizontal beam resting on the earth. The whole of the south end of my cottage, the central partition wall, and two-thirds of the west side, was resting on the soil until a few years ago. We frequently had plants coming through from outside and trying to grow through cracks in the floor. On one occasion we had a mole — only for a short while. Round the rest of the building there runs a low brick wall, varying in height from eighteen inches to a single layer of bricks. It is clear that the south and west part of the house is older than the rest, having been left in position when the rest was re-built. The re-building, there is reason to suppose, was done about 1580. When was the older part built? With no documentary evidence to assist my speculation, I estimated a gap of something less than a hundred years, and settled for c. 1490. When I did later discover some documentary evidence, I was intrigued to find that I was only ten years wide of the mark.

The roof likewise has its tale to tell. Not the thatch; that is what it always was: solidly packed and skilfully secured wheat straw; much thicker now than it used to be, and protected by wire, without which its life would be reduced from thirty years to about ten, as it used to be. No, I mean the rafters on which the thatch sits, and which play their part in holding the frame together. It is clear that the tie-beams have been removed at some time and set higher up, to provide more head-room. The original loft or chamber did not require much head-room, being used solely for storage. Virtually the whole roof was reconstructed, for only eight of the original rafters are still there. Many of the "new" rafters were not shaped in any way; they are branches taken straight from the tree, still with much of the bark on them, and not very straight either.

The windows, as one would expect, have undergone a good deal of alteration. Most are in the original position, or nearly so, and some are no bigger now than were the original windows. The biggest alteration is illustrated in my sketch (Fig. 4).

When we came here there were two snags — (there were dozens, actually, most of which disappeared with time, usage and a little ingenuity) — two real snags. One was the huge ten-inch beam spanning the living-room ceiling already mentioned. The other was access to the bedroom above that ceiling. Having mounted the stairs, in itself something of an acrobatic feat, one is confronted by a barrier some sixteen inches high, the top of it being a stout tie-beam, one of four spanning the width of the frame. Stepping over this, one then steps down, twenty inches this time, to reach the bedroom floor, feet first with any luck. The drop on the inside was eased by the insertion of a half-way step, but there is little one can do about the step up on the outside, except get used to it.

We got so used to it that for long enough I gave the matter no further thought beyond reflecting that the man who built the cottage must have been either a very small or a very stupid man. Of course he was neither. When you look more closely, it becomes obvious that that huge beam, along with its supports, and the twenty-six short beams and their supports, have nothing to do with the structural frame of the house. The whole lot could be taken out, leaving the living-room open to the roof, as it once was; also depriving me of a bedroom! When was this floor (or ceiling, according to whether you are upstairs or down) inserted? "Bedrooms" were unknown in Tudor houses of this class, in Tudor times. During the great building boom of Elizabethan days most yeomen's houses were built with one "chamber", and a second or third was added to most of them during the next hundred years or so. These chambers were intended primarily as store-rooms, only secondarily as sleeping-rooms; no doubt they frequently served both purposes at once. The yeoman's first and most constant concern was for his wealth – wool, saffron, seed-corn, cheese etc.; commodities too precious to be kept in the barn, where they would have been too much of a temptation, and too easy a prey, to rogues and vagabonds. When, a few years ago, I laboriously cleaned out the spaces between the 16" floorboards in this chamber, I found many grains of wheat and barley embedded in the dirt, where they had lain for some three hundred years. The insertion of the floor can be dated with fair accuracy to c. 1620. It looks "Elizabethan", but it isn't. It is but one of many examples of style outliving period.

The other bedroom or "chamber" is clearly older. Its floor-beams are a complete hotch-potch; some are just straightish branches, one was obviously once a wall-plate, one is half-burnt, some are half-trimmed; only one actually looks like a beam, and that was put in thirty-five years ago. There has been more repairing done here than in any other part of the house. Access to this chamber originally can only have been by ladder, in the S.E. corner.

To sum up, then, there are three stages within the present structure:

(i) A late medieval house consisting of hall, parlour, and one chamber; one door, few windows, and those very small; earth floor; perhaps with a fireplace, perhaps not. The kitchen was in all probability a separate building at the north end.

(ii) A sixteenth-century house with hall, parlour, one chamber; fireplace with brick chimney; kitchen behind the chimney-stack; the same small windows; two doors; earth floor.

(iii) A seventeenth-century house with hall, parlour, two chambers, kitchen, larger windows, brick floors and a staircase. And that is how it remained, with the addition of a brick oven, for over three hundred years.

I have refrained from cataloguing all the many peg-holes, mortices, grooves about the place; they are too numerous. Nor have I told in detail the story of the doors, all of which were once capable of being locked, bolted and barred, evidence that the Englishman's home was indeed his castle.

There only remains to explain one thing before I tell the story proper. I have called the house a "cottage", and shall continue to do so. But the word is a misnomer, as is "villa", "residence" etc. Properly speaking, there is no such thing as a Tudor cottage today. The cottage or "cot" of Tudor times was an insubstantial affair which could be erected in a day and dismantled in a few hours. It was not intended to last much more than the life of the man who erected it, and that man was invariably a poor man. What we call today a "Tudor cottage" was built as a

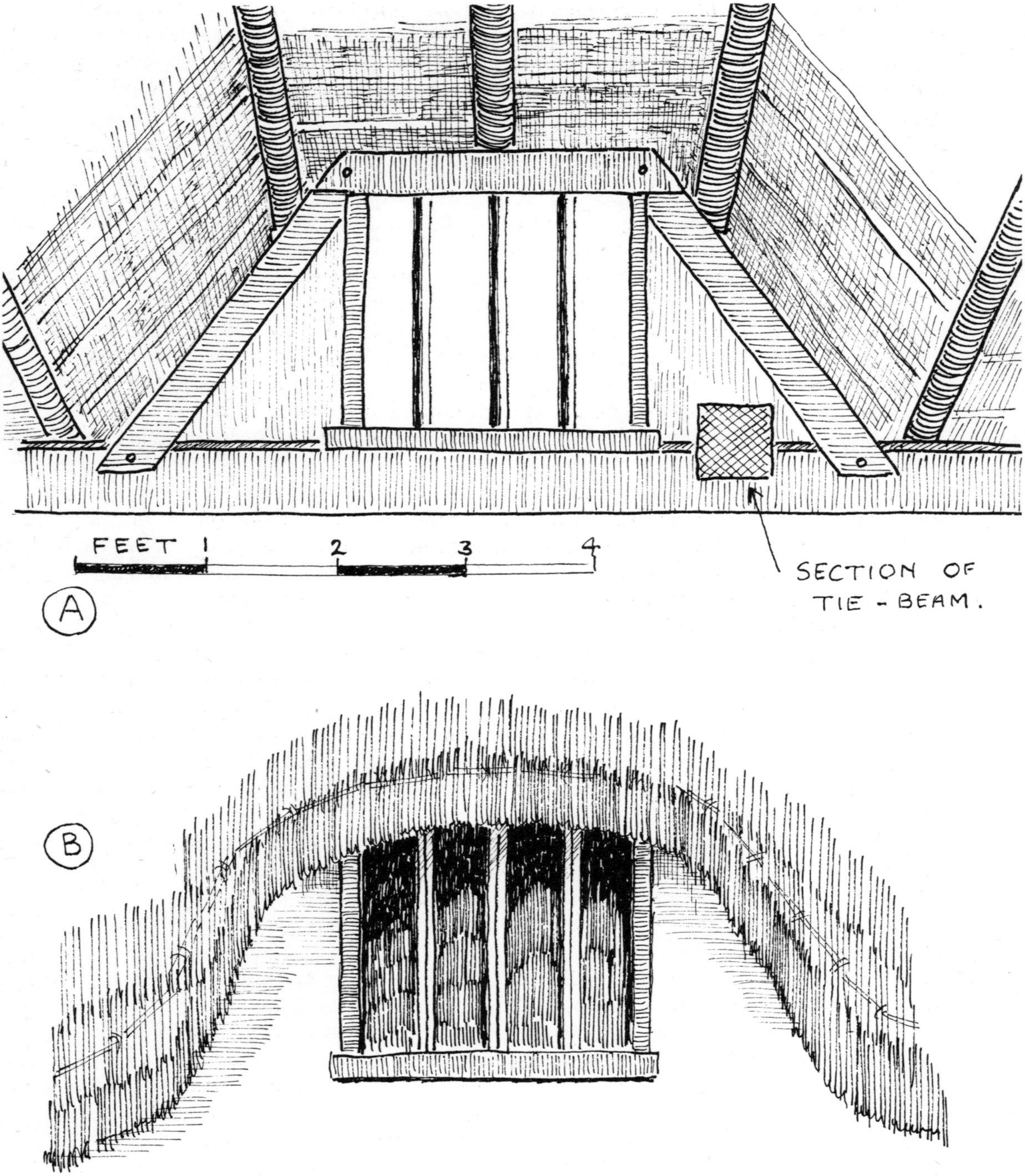

Fig. 4 The original east window, from the inside (A) and outside (B).

house, the house of a yeoman or merchant. I will not say that it was intended to last 400 years, but the fact is that many of them have, so sturdily were they built. It was built by and for a well-to-do man. These yeomen, as I hope to show, were in the main men whose chief assets were a spirit of sturdy independence, common-sense, thrift, and an unflinching acceptance of hard work as one of the necessities of life. Comfort, privacy, status-seeking, labour-saving were things unknown to them, and unsought by them. True, some of them aspired to be "gentlemen"; some of them, very few, achieved that aim. Most were obviously content with their lot and had no pretentions to anything better. Their houses were small, but big enough for their needs. So long as the house was dry, warm, firm and safe, what else mattered?

CHAPTER III
From Domesday to St. George

I am not going to pretend that I have traced the history of my cottage back to 1066! But I can confidently narrate a good deal about the site on which it stands, and about the men who owned the site, a narrative which, however sketchy, takes us back even earlier than the eleventh century.

The shape and size of the village, shape which it was to retain for a thousand years until the growth in size made a change in shape inevitable, were determined in mid-Saxon times by the digging of the Town Ditch. At the western end of the village the ditch began its southerly curve round the base of West Hill, while the main street curved slightly northward. Both were cut across by an ancient way running north-south from the river-crossings at Barrington to the Icknield Way. The apex of the triangle thus formed became the Green. The middle of it formed an obvious site for a house occupying an unique situation. There can be no doubt at all that this site, now occupied by my cottage, was occupied by a house when the village began its existence. As regards the "socmen", "villeins", "bordars" or "cottars" who lived here throughout five centuries, I know nothing. I know something about the men to whom they paid their rents, for whom they performed services, and at whose hands they received both protection and persecution.

Before the Norman Conquest the land was owned — "held" would perhaps be a more accurate term — by a Saxon called Sigar. He was evidently a man of some diplomatic talent, for, when his overlord Asgar was killed at the Battle of Hastings, and his holdings transferred to Geoffrey de Mandeville, Sigar was left in possession of his holdings, with Geoffrey as his new overlord. He was one of the few Saxons to retain their lands, and his was a very fair estate of about 560 acres, lying three parts in Foxton, one part in Shepreth. When Sigar died, he was succeeded by a Frenchman. The Mandevilles continued as overlords, and, like the rest of the wicked barons, indulged freely in political intrigue and rapacity. One of them, another Sir Geoffrey, embarked finally upon a career of out-and-out plunder which was terminated by a chance arrow at the siege of Burwell Castle in 1142. Twenty years later his brother William, for the good of his soul, granted £5 annually from the revenues of his manor of Foxton and Shepreth to the Preceptor of the Hospital of the Knights of St. John of Jerusalem, situated at Shingay. It would be inspiring to think that this plot of ground made its contribution, however small, to that series of enterprises, part religious, part rapacious, part political and part sheer lunacy, known as the Crusades. The link is undoubtedly there. In actual fact the chief beneficiary was William de Mandeville, for by virtue of the gift the manor was exempt from "scutage", i.e. the fee payable in lieu of military service.

For the greater part of the 12th century the land was held by Alan de Shepreth and his family. Soon after 1200, Alan's daughter Petronilla married William de la Haye, taking the manor with her as dowry. The De la Haye family, living at the Hallyards in Shepreth, held the manor, and everything else on which they could lay hands, for the next 150 years. The Hundred Roll of 1288 gives the first detailed description of the De la Haye estate in Foxton; 25 houses and 344 acres of land, paying an annual total of £4. 15s. 8d. in rents and £5. 16s. 3d. worth of services. Which of those houses was the one occupying this site I cannot say with any certainty, but circumstances point strongly to the possibility that it was the house of Ralph Karesey, who held a house and 40 acres of land of the De la Haye manor, besides holding 3 roods of meadow of Mortimer's manor, and another house and one acre of the Chatteris manor. Ralph persistently refused to pay homage at the manor-court of the Abbess of Chatteris, an action wholly in keeping with the animosity which existed between the various manors and their tenants.

In 1324, John de la Haye secured from Edward II a grant of the right to hold a fair in Foxton, and for the next five hundred and eighty-six years it continued to be held on the Green, just in front of this house. The Mortimers had already, in 1310, been granted the right to hold a fair at the other end of the village. Rid your mind of any idea about swings and roundabouts and coconut-shies; the fairs were purely for trading purposes, and their main reason for coming into being was that the tolls paid by the stall-holders made a useful addition to manorial revenue. John de la Haye did not take kindly to competition. In 1337 he and his armed ruffians broke up the Mortimer fair, overturning the booths and forbidding the taking of tolls. We are not told whether this was a reprisal for similar action by William Mortimer, or whether it provoked similar action in its turn. We may be sure that the three-day fair, held around the Feast of St. Lawrence, was always the occasion of loud bargaining, hard drinking and a good deal of coarse merrymaking.

In the mid-fourteenth century the manor again changed hands for want of male heirs. Margaret de la Haye married John Dengayne. Sir John in 1356 was granted licence of free warren on his manor, which meant that he could "hunt" foxes, badgers, hares, rabbits, pheasants, partridges, herons, wild cats – anything, in fact, except deer and wild boar. At the same time he was confirmed in his right to hold a fair, and also a weekly market. The "grene" then became, and for some 200 years continued to be, the "Merketstede" (market-place). It is doubtful whether the market ever had much commercial importance, and certain that it conferred no special status upon the village. Almost every village in the neighbourhood had a market; the amount of trading to be done can never have justified their existence; nor can there ever have been a surplus of produce such as could not be disposed of by internal barter. Moreover, conditions of travelling, coupled with the decline in population which set in before the market was even established, must have resulted in a very sparse attendance.

The market did serve one useful purpose, however, in that it provided a time and place at which public pronouncements could be made concerning impounded animals, rogues and vagabonds, meetings of the manor-court, and such royal proclamations as filtered thus far down the scale of administration. And the market-place was the obvious location of that instrument of rough justice, the stocks, which stood there, constantly repaired and renewed, until the end of the 18th century. I can find no evidence of the existence of a ducking-stool, though there is any amount of evidence pointing to a regular supply of slanderous females (why only females?) who might have kept it in employment. If it did exist, it would certainly have been sited on the Green, for there was an ample supply of clean water in the form of the Town Brook. True, ducks and washing of clothes in the

Fig. 5 The brass of Baldwin St. George in Hatley Church. 1425.

Brook were expressly banned by local edict, but the rules could have been temporarily waived in the interests of "justice".

When Sir John Dengayne died he left only two daughters, Joan and Mary, as coheiresses, and the manor was divided between them. This was the beginning of the fragmentation which continued throughout two centuries, and caused such confusion to Layer, Cole, Lysons and, finally, me. Joan Dengayne in 1382 married Baldwin St. George. It was not exactly what you might call a love-match. Baldwin stipulated that Sir John should pay him 150 marks (a mark was 13/4), 40 before the marriage and the rest secured by a "statute of the staple". (Sheep and wool have always played a big part in the history of this house.) Baldwin for his part was to settle two other manors on his bride. If Sir John should fail in any of the payments, then Baldwin should "be at choice for the said marriage, whether he will or no". Well, the marriage did take place, and the St. Georges had a good innings as lords of the half-manor.

Baldwin's name has survived to posterity in two ways. It is borne — or was until a few years ago — by a small triangular piece of land lying between the Shepreth Brook and what was the Town Brook: "Baldwin's Close". This was one of the earliest enclosures outside the immediate village area, and was undoubtedly made as a sanctuary for rabbits. Not with any view to ensuring the safety of the rabbits, merely to ensure that they were there when Baldwin wanted them. The area in the vicinity of the close was for long known as the "Conniger" or "Connigree" (rabbit-warren) and, until the advent of myxomatosis wiped them out, there was no better spot for catching rabbits.

The other of Baldwin's survivals is in the form of a commemorative brass in Hatley church. It bears the date 1425, and if that is the date of his death he must have been well over ninety when he died. For he was "admitted to the first tonsure", along with his brother Richard, at Ditton in 1341. The brass is in no sense a portrait; it shows, as most of them do, an armour-clad knight in the prime of life, dog at feet. The succession of plagues in the 14th century, in particular the Black Death of 1349, seems to have left the St. George family singularly untouched. They were an exceptionally pious family. Their immunity, however, was probably due not so much to this as to the isolation of their manor of Hungry Hatley. No such immunity was enjoyed by the occupants of this cottage; the plague had set foot inside the door, and was not to be easily dislodged.

The half-manor descended to Baldwin's son John; then to William; then to Richard. Sir Richard was the husband of Lady Ann St. George who came to live in Foxton in 1511, by which date we are in a position to relegate the manorial owners of this cottage into the background, and concentrate on the occupiers.

CHAPTER IV
Peppercorns

My story, as regards the documented history of this house and its occupants, begins with the ducks. I was not thinking of the ducks as occupants of the house, though it would seem that such a possibility is not to be ruled out. In 1492 the Court Leet of the Manor of Foxton Bury, which had jurisdiction over all who lived in Foxton, whether tenants or not, decreed that:

> "No tenant or resident within the precincts of this court shall allow his ducks or geese to be or go in the common brook running through the middle of this village, but shall either sell them or keep them within their tenements and houses, on pain of a fine of 3/4 for each offence."

They had been issuing such orders for about three hundred years, perhaps longer, and would continue to do so for another three hundred years, until such time as the Town Brook ceased to be the sole supply of drinking-water for the village. Like all the other by-laws made by the manor-court, it was as much honoured in the breach as in the observance. In 1495:

> "John Fuller, John Rogers, John Skep, Katherine Baret, John Lawe, John Everard, John Spenser and Richard Pepercorn allowed their ducks to go and remain in the common brook running through the village, causing serious nuisance and contrary to previous orders, and each offender shall forfeit 6d."

The difference between the threatened penalty and the one actually imposed is easily explained. All but two of the offenders were members of the jury! All were resident in the west end of the village. Only one was not a tenant of the Bury manor – Richard Pepercorn.

He next attracted the attention of the court on Oct. 17th 1501, when:

> " – they say that Richard Pepercorn obstructed the paths leading from le Merketstede; he is therefore ordered to amend the matter before the Feast of the Nativity next, under pain of a fine of 6/8, by verdict of the whole court."

That gives us an exact date for the construction of the house. No other activity could have caused such an obstruction for so long. The house stood on the very edge of the market-place, and Richard had no choice but to hinder the weekly business – such as there was – when laying out and assembling the timbers prior to "raising" the frame. Later there would be two or three loads of straw lying there for a few weeks whilst the thatch was being put on. The demolition of the old house would also require some room for the sorting-out of timbers to be re-used, as many were. The work was finished by Christmas, and so well done that about a quarter of it is still standing today.

Old Richard, with the help of his three sons, had at last realised what had no doubt been a dream for many years. Then, having got his new house, he died. Time and time again this happens in the story of these ordinary people; they work and slave and save all their lives, settle down at last to enjoy the fruits of their labour, then "snip" – Fate cuts the thread. It seems a bit unfair. Don't forget, though, that those bones which Richard buried in the floor were intended for the house, not for him.

Fig. 6 Richard Peppercorn "obstructed the paths leading from the Marketplace."

Richard's eldest son William inherited the house, and lived here with his mother Alice, then later with his wife and family. How much land he farmed I do not know. Not enough for his needs, that I do know. His chief lack was pasture to graze his animals, a lack which at this time was felt by the whole village, and which was to become ever more acute. The right to graze the "commons", which included the common fields lying fallow, the wastes, the meadows in winter etc., was jealously guarded by those men already established, and was granted in proportion to the amount of arable land which a man farmed. William, holding no land of the Bury, had no "common rights" of the Bury. His horses did not understand this. In 1507:

> "William Pepyrcorne is daily a transgressor in the cornfields of the tenants there with his horses, and is fined xx d."

The horses landed up in the manor pound, whence William retrieved them. One could not work without horses; nor could one wait for the constable and the proper course of the law:

> "The said William broke the pound of the manor in taking an animal impounded for trespass in the corn of Lady Tanfield. Fined xii d."

An expensive business; and it went on:

> "1515. William Pepercorn, it is reported, broke le pynfolde of the Lady. Fined xii d."

His only remedy lay in acquiring some Bury land. In 1517 he at last succeeded:

> "John Porter alienated (William, as tenant of another manor, was an "alien") to William Pepercorne one XVIII acre Ware Land (the origin of "ware" land is unknown; it is clearly, however, an original allocation appertaining to a tenement or house, possibly half a virgate, i.e. sixteen acres; all acreages at this time are purely nominal) lying in the fields of Foxton in various pieces, once Thomas Porter's, called William Shepards, which same John Porter here in court surrenders to the use of the said William Pepercorne who present in court is admitted tenant, to hold to him his heirs and assigns by the rod (the ancient symbol of authority) at the will of the Lady (of the Manor) according to the custom of the manor at the ancient rent (rents remained unchanged for centuries) and services (there were none by this time, but this bit of the formula was not abandoned for another 200 years) due therefor. And for having the statutory title thereto he gives (note that it is a "gift", not an exaction) to the Lady by way of entry-fine x s. (roughly one year's rent; it was to increase sharply before long) and he did fealty (another archaic survival without any real significance any longer)."

William's mother died here in 1519. Her will provides a glimpse into the cottage, some details about the farming of the day, and some idea of the pious nature of the old lady. Regarding the latter, it needs to be borne in mind that the preamble to the will is standard formula. Here it is, quoted in full, with the original spelling, punctuation added:

> In the name of god amen. The yere of our Lord god MCCCCC & XIX the XXIXth day of Novembre, I, Alice Pepircorne of ffoxton, hole of mynd & of good memory, make my testament & laste Will in forme foloinge. Inprimis I bequeathe my soule to godd almighty, to his mother saunte Mary and to the

holy company of hevyn, my body to be buried in the churchyard of Saunte Laurent in ffoxton beforesaide. Also I bequeathe to the high altare in the saide church of ffoxton ii bushells of barley. Also I bequeathe to the Rodelofte in the saide church oon quarter barley. Item to the torches ii bushelles barley. Item to Sainte Anne light ii bushelles barley. Item to the belles ii bushellis barley. Item to Alexandre my sonn oon quarter barley. Item to Edward my sonn ii quarters barley. Item to the same Edward oon brasse pan, oon paire shetis, the oon of towe, the other flaxen. Item I bequeth to Saincte Anne gilde oon table clothe flaxen. Item to Edward my sonn oon table clothe. Item I bequeth to Alice Shopman my best gowne. Item to Alexandre my sonnys wif oon grene gowne. Item I Will that my Vicare have viii d. for to say ii massis for my husband & me. Item I Will to the chirche of ffoxton too halfe shetis for to make ii altare clothis. Also I Will that William Pepircorne my sonn shalbe myn Executore, he to dispose my goodis not bequeathed in deads of charite & to kepe oon obite in the church of ffoxton yerly during the lif of the saide William. And when it shall please god that the saide William shall departe this present lif, than he to delyver to the church gardianys of ffoxton ii bolocks price of xx s. or ellis xx s. sterling of good and lawfull money of England, they therwith to kepe the forsaid obite. Also I Will that oon Roode safron & oon Carte goo to the performance of this saide obite. Thes being Witnes: Master Richard Brekenhed, Vicar, Sir ffrauncis Lancaster, prest, Jhon Humfray and other specially desired to the same.

The "obit" was an annual service intended to keep alive the memory of the benefactor. The price paid for this perpetuity seems rather high, when masses could be had for fourpence each – but it was "for ever". Alice could not know that, in a few years' time, the Reformation was to sweep away masses for the soul, obits, indulgences and the like, as well as St. Anne's Guild.

Saffron deserves a word of comment here, particularly as it will recur in wills for the next two centuries. The saffron crocus was cultivated in small plots, usually of ¼, ½ or 1 acre, occupying the same ground for three years. The yellow stamens were collected and made into powder used for flavouring foodstuffs (cakes and biscuits mostly) also for colouring some materials. It was a very profitable crop, especially suitable to small-scale farming.

William Pepercorn, now married and with three small daughters of his own in addition to the three children of his wife by her first marriage, had his hands full. He still found time to attend the manor-court as one of the homage, and had his share of extra duties.

1521. And it is likewise ordered that William Pepercorne, William Foster, William Rayner, Thomas Wells, John Raymond, John Skynner and Richard Newman shall make and adequately clean out the common brook from the house of Thomas Barrett as far as the manor of Mortimers before the Feast of the Nativity of St. John Baptist next, on pain of each forfeiting 6/8 to the Lady."

But that was one duty which he failed to perform, for it had pleased God that he should "departe this present lif." He was a fit man when he wrote his will, but within a year he was dead, stricken by that mysterious plague which lingered on, to flare up every now and then with sudden, cruel violence. His will is even more illuminating than that of his mother:

"In the name of god Amen. The xviiith day of October in the yere of our Lorde MCCCCCXX And in the xiith yere of King Henry the VIIIth, I, William Pepercorne of ffoxton — being of hole mynde and good memorie — first I bequeth my soule to allmighty god, to our lady Seynt Mary and to all the seynts of hevyn — Also I bequeth to the high awter of my parishe Cherche for my tithes and offering negligently forgoten xx d. Item, to the Rodeloft one quarter of barly. Item to the bellys ii busshells barly. Item to the torches ii busshells Barly. Item to Seynt Annes Guylde ii busshells Barly. Item I will that xxx ii. masses be said for my soule and all cristen soules after my decease at a conveniant tyme shortly after my deth. Item I wille that Avys, Agnes and Anne my iii doughters have every of them v quarters of Barly. And they and ther stoke to remayne in the keping of Johane my wiff to nuresse. And if it fortune any of them to discease within age, that than the said stoke to be departed betwyne them the overlyvers. Item, I geve to John Hogekyn my wiffes sonne a shode Carte, to be delyvered to hym at suche tyme as he shalbe able to occupy husbandry him selfe. And also ii quarters of Barly to sow his lond at his first occupying. Item, I geve to Margarett Hogekyng my Wiffs doughter one quarter of Barly and one yong milche bullock. Item, I geve to Johane Hokeking my Wiffs other doughter one quarter of Barly. Item I will that Johan my wif shall have my Copyhold called Shepards in ffoxton as long as she conteneth single and unmarried. And if she marye, that than immediatly I will that ye said Copy be solde be my Executrice and the money therof comying I bequeth xxvi s. viii d. to bye an Abbe and a vestament with the pertinens to my parishe Cherche of ffoxton. And the Residue of the money to be disposed in masses and other charitable deds of almes for the helth of my soule and all cristen soulls. Item I wille that my Executrice after my decease content and pay to the Cherche Wardens of the said ffoxton xx s. or ii bullocks price of xx s. And they to kepe yerely the yeremynd of Alis Pepercorne my mother according as it is in her wille. Item I will that suche Implements and stuff of housholde that was late Alys my mothers be devided among Avis, Agnes and Anne my iii Doughters. Item I will and geve my *Copy that I holde of my Lady Seynt George* in ffoxton to Johan my wiff terme of her liff and after her decease to Agnes my Doughter. The Residue of my goods not bequethed, my detts first payed and my legacis performed, I geve and bequeth to Johan my Wyff Whome I make & ordeyne my Executrice alone. Witnesses being present viz. Thomas Feyrle, Richard Newman, Thomas Wells, William Foster with dyverse moo."

William had married another man's widow, yet he did not wish his widow to marry again! This feature arises again and again in wills of this period. I cannot explain it, other than as an illustration of the determination to keep property in the family. Joan was confirmed in her possession of the land on the condition stipulated, at the next session of the court, and paid the fee of 6/8. But how could a widow with six children, five of them young girls, manage a farm of some 40 acres? Impossible. A husband had to be found, and found quickly. Joan must have been an attractive woman, besides possessing an attractive house and land, for, those six children notwithstanding, she had married again, for the third time, within a year of William's death. Then there was that awkward clause in the will to be circumvented. John Sympton and Joan his wife, lately wife of William Pepercorne, came to the manor-court on April 29th 1523. The Steward had sought the advice of the Abbess, this being a matter wherein Canon Law was as much involved as Civil Law, and a satisfactory solution was found. John and Joan were allowed to keep the land (for a further fee of 8/-).

"On the following condition, viz. that the said John and Joan shall pay or cause to be paid four marks — as follows, i.e. to the churchwardens of Foxton at the Feast of the Exaltation of the Holy Cross next, for the use of the said church, xxvi s. viii d., and paying and distributing the other xxvi s. viii d. for the celebration of masses and doing charitable works at the discretion of the said Joan for the soul of the said William Pepercorne in the best and quickest way she can within two years from now — And if she shall default in paying the said four marks — then it shall be right and proper for the Lady to retake possession of the said land."

So John and Joan settled down happily, and with easy consciences, on the farm. Joan had two more children, a girl and a boy. Do not waste your time in wondering how a family of two adults and eight children managed to live in a small house of three rooms. Larger families than that have been reared in smaller houses than this. Anyway, some of the children were getting near to marriageable age. Besides, the more mouths there were to feed, the more hands there were to work.

John Sympton for a number of years served the village as one of the ale-tasters, the only official duty which was eagerly sought and performed. And right well he did the job. Unlike most holders of that office, he was never fined for not doing his duty. Indeed he was somewhat over-zealous for the good ladies who eked out a living by selling ale — Joan Wells, Isabella Virley and Joan Rayner. They tried to thwart him by offering their ale for sale before he had had an opportunity to test it and set a price on it. John, backed by the court, put a stop to that.

Meanwhile the family grew up. Agnes Pepercorn married Robert Wells, and in 1540 she and her husband sued John Sympton for a third part of the eighteen-acre ware called Will Shepherds. The Reformation had now happened, and there was some doubt, Robert hoped, about the validity of the settlement made by the former Abbess of Chatteris. John was summoned to court, but ignored the order. Possession was nine points of the law, validity or no validity. Then the two other girls married, Alice (Avys) to Henry Freeman, Anne to Roger Ellis. All three made another attempt in 1543 to get hold of the land. Again the case was postponed, and again John Sympton summoned to appear. He had by this time answered a more imperious summons — he was dead. The girls and their husbands never did get the land. Joan Sympton hung on to it until such time as she had to hand it over to her son John in 1559.

After the death of her third husband and the departure of all the daughters, Joan continued to live here with son John (until he married) and followed the usual practice by becoming a seller of ale and bread, for which trade her house was ideally situated, despite the fact that the weekly market had now ceased to exist. For fifteen years the old lady carried on, until well into her seventies. Every year she was fined, sums varying from 3d. to 10d., for breaking the assise of bread and ale. It is more than likely that, towards the end, she could scarcely see what she was supposed to be measuring and weighing. On one occasion at least it was her own son-in-law who prosecuted her. She died in about 1560 (her death is not recorded). Her daughter Agnes Wells inherited the house, for which she had no use. The Wells family already owned three other houses. It was obviously sold, perhaps even before old Joan died. And the new owner was called Campion.

CHAPTER V
One Campion, A Yeoman

A little more manorial history is called for here, to fill in the background. Lady Anne St. George had inherited one half of the former De la Haye manor. (The other half acquired the name of Wimbish, from John Wimbish, who in 1426 had married Margery Blyton, daughter of Mary Dengayne, and has kept the name ever since, though once more split into Foxton and Shepreth elements.) Anne St. George, eldest daughter of Lady Anne, married John Docwra in 1517, and inherited the half-manor on the death of her mother in 1524, whereupon the name of "Docwra's" was bestowed upon it, and so it has remained. John Docwra acquired other manors at Temple Dinsley and Putteridge, and transferred his main interests to Hertfordshire. His son Thomas inherited the estates, and built the house at Shepreth still called "Docwra's Manor". His interest in it was short-lived, however. According to the scanty records available, only one manor-court was held there in his name, in 1565, "for the manor of Shepreth".

It seems certain that, in 1565 or just before, both halves of the original manor were divided into quarters. The Foxton half of the Wimbish half was bought by Richard Warren, who bought Foxton Bury at the same time. The Foxton half of the Docwra half was bought by "one Campion, a yeoman" and Philip Welbore, whilst one Hancock bought the Shepreth half. So that the owner of this house was the owner of one eighth of the original manor. Whether that entitles me to claim for the house the status of "manor house", I am not very sure. The truth is, I suspect, that the manor technically ceased to be a manor once the fragmentation went beyond the first split. This was John Layer's view, and he was a lawyer. He was also a snob, who had no intention of hobnobbing with yeomen claiming to be lords of manors. Anyway, let us consider the Campions, "mean" though they may have been.

Simon Campion came from Thriplow to Foxton in 1546, when he bought a house just down the road from here, together with about 26 acres of land. This entitled him to a say on the homage or "jury" of the manor-court, which he attended regularly for the next 16 years. His name soon appears at the head of the list, a sure indication that he was a man of substance, a leading citizen. He served as constable at least once, and as churchwarden for a number of years. At some time before 1554 he acquired the copyhold of this house and of the other Docwra house which stood where the Black Boy was to stand later. (See map, Fig. 9). This is attested by the fact that in 1554

> "The Bailiff was ordered to summon Simon Campyon to make a certain way at Conylande with a gate as often as it shall be necessary."

The responsibility for erecting gates across roads, a vital necessity under the open-field system, was always thrust upon individuals whenever possible.

It is almost certain that Simon came to live here when Joan Sympton died; it is quite certain that he would not have evicted the old lady before she died – such a thing was simply not done. His son Thomas lived in the house down the road, his son John in the house across the Green. He died here in 1563, a wealthy man by village standards, and very conscious of his wealth, which he measured in "quarters" of barley (a quarter meant quarter of a ton, nominally, i.e. 2 sacks; there was not then, as there is not now, any standard relationship between weight and measure in corn). Here is the substance of his will, far too long and verbose to be quoted in full:

"In the name of god amen. The 30th Aguste in the yeare – 1562 – I, Symon Campion of Foxton – husbondman – to Nicholas my Sonne xx quarters of barlye – within the space of two yeares – to John Campion my Sonne xx quarters of barlye – within two yeares – item I will that my Sonne John shall have the howses and lands that I have at Thriploe bothe of free and coppie – to Margaret my Daughter fyve quarters of barlye to be paide all in one yeare – and also to Ellen my Daughter other fyve quarters – to Johanna Bawdricke my daughter fyve quarters of barlye paide out of this yeres croppe. And also I will she have the beste bullocks in my yarde excepte two – to Alice Marlay fyve quarters of barlye and one bullocke – at the age of xxi yeres or at the daye of her marriage – to John Richarde thre quarters barlye – And to Cycelie my maide one quarter barlye – to John Melwood my Servante one quarter barlye – And to John Chapman my Servante iii s. iiii d. – to Lambert my Servant one quarter barlye at the age of xxi yeres and to John Welles my sarvant xiid. – to every one of my godchildren xiid. in monye – to Thomasyne my Sonne Thomas his wyffes Daughter fyve quarters of barlye – at the daye of her marriage. And to Elizabethe Bawdricke other fyve quarters of barlye – to every one of my childrens children that now be borne and be alyve, one quarter of barlye a pece. Item – that in casse be my Sonne Thomas do decease without any hiere malle of his bodye lawfully begotten (then follows a most elaborate series of provisos – all in vain because Thomas did have a male heir) – to Peter Roger of Babram one quarter barlye – the residue of all my goods – to Thomas Campion my Sonne to paye my Debts and legacies and to bringe me honestlye to the ground and to bestowe them in deeds of charitie as he thinketh beste to the plesure of god."

Even when those twenty tons of barley had been paid out, Thomas Campion's heritage was a very handsome one. He had inherited, along with the houses and land, his father's character and his father's respected status. He in his turn appears at the head of the list of homage, and served as churchwarden for several years. When the Docwra estate came on the market, Thomas bought up as much as he could, about 40 acres of land and two houses, including this house. He would pay no more rent; that part of the manor which he occupied was now his own. It is almost certain that he came to live here after Simon's death. His first wife died young, leaving him with one daughter, delightfully named Thomasyne. He married again, and had three children by his second wife.

Then something went wrong with the affairs of Thomas Campion. Something went very wrong with the nature of Thomas Campion. Whether it was that his head was turned by worldly success; whether he tried to be "Lord of the Manor" and met with nothing but ridicule; or whether his second marriage turned out all wrong – I do not know. But the prosaic facts in the records concerning him make it clear that he became arrogant, quarrelsome and anything but a respected citizen.

He began, in 1566, by refusing to attend the first court of Sir Richard Warren, at the Bury, though he did consent in later years to attend as one of the homage for Wimbish. In 1571, summoned to the Bury court, he refused to take the oath, "Showing contempt of court and setting a bad example to the others", for which he was fined 20/-. The same year he enclosed a piece of land called Horsecroft, stealing some of his neighbours' land, was fined 12d. and ordered to set back his fence or face a fine of 40/-. The order was repeated several times, without compliance on the part of Thomas, and in 1576 he was fined 40/-. At the same court he was fined 3/4 for ploughing 1½ acres in Downfield. Five of his neighbours were arraigned on the same charge — "land-grabbing" at the expense of the common pasture. Not surprisingly, drinking and gambling come into the picture.

1576. George Awder, John Fuller, Thomas Campion, Will Austyn, Will Fuller and Will Cock played illegal games. Each fined 4d.

Margaret Sympton permitted illicit gaming in her house, playing for drinks. Fined 6d.

(I hate to say it, but George Awder was the vicar!)

Thomas was by no means the only arrogant thruster in the village. There were half a dozen at least, all competing for the role of "top dog", a state of affairs which would not have existed had there been a resident squire to act as indisputable leader. In the matter of petty transgression there was no one to equal John Rayner, and it was inevitable that a clash between him and Thomas should come eventually, and that when it came it should concern boundaries. Thomas won his case, and John kept the trees which were in dispute.

The entries on the court-rolls tend to become tantalisingly cryptic just when one most needs a full and clear statement. On May 3rd 1581 the first item of business dealt with is recorded thus:

"The said jurors present that Thomas Campyon is a transgressor with his pond. Therefore he is fined xiid."

The Clerk and Steward were concerned solely with recording and collecting that shilling due from Thomas. I would like to know exactly where and why he made that pond. I am almost certain that it was connected with the rebuilding of this house and the re-designing of the layout of the farm. I am sure that Thomas rebuilt the house in 1580. Most of what he built is still standing today, just as he built it. The old house was not in a bad condition, indeed much of it was so sound that he left it in position, and that bit too still stands. Why did he rebuild, then? There were two reasons. One was that he wanted a good brick chimney and fireplace, instead of the outside kitchen. The other was, quite simply, that everybody else was building. The latter part of the reign of the first Queen Elizabeth saw the biggest boom in rural housing that the country had ever known, or was to know again until the days of the second Queen Elizabeth.

Having built his "new" house, and settled in it, Thomas Campion died. I do not know his age; he was certainly not "old". His will, quoted below, reveals some interesting facts, and presents a pretty problem.

"In the name of god Amen. This 11th daye of November — 1581. I, Thomas Campyon, beinge whole of mynd and good memorye — all other wills by writings or by word of mouthe disaloweinge and sett apart — Item — unto my twoe sones Nycholas Campyon and William Campyon all my land as well free as coppy that I have nowe — in the parish of Foxton, with all howses and tenements that I doe nowe injoye, uppon this condicion, that my land be fyrst lett for certaine yeres to paye oute of yt one Hundrede Poundes to Mr. Fletcher uppon the Feast of St. Michaell Arckangell next — to Katherine Campyon my daugher £30 — within halfe a yere after my departinge — to Katherine my daughter a hutche with certeine lynen and wollen to the valewe of £10 — to Katherine my daughter twoe beast at her choice and one aker of saffran, halfe of newe ground and halfe of the ould, the best bedd in the house with all that belonge to yt, the greate brasse pott with twoe of the best kettles, and thretye Poundes of pewter — to Thomas Morley fyve seive barley, halfe an Aker of saffron, the halfe to be newe ground, the halfe ould land — to John Caldcott twoe seive barley, an Ewe and a lambe and xiis. of monye which I owe hym — to Margaret Borowe my maid twoe seive of barley and xliiis. iiiid. I owe unto her — to Johanna Gibsone twoe seive barley and one ewe and a lambe — to Symon Campyn of Thriplowe one seive barley — to Thomas Rogers of Pampisford one seive barley — to Thomas Campyon of Babram one seive barley — to Willyam Campyon of Babrom one seive barley — unto my twoe sones Nicholas and William, whome I make my sole executors joyntlye togither the Rest of all my goodes as well corne as cattle with all houshold stuffe that I now injoye or ought to injoye, my debtes and legacies fyrste discharged. And this I make my last will and Testament willinge my twoe brothers to be governers and guides for my twoe sones, and they to have for there paines xxs. a pece. In witness to this; William Awsten, George Brian, Thomas Marley, John Caldcott."

It is to be noted, firstly, that Thomas was very much in debt, having had to borrow money even from his maid, though he had plenty of relatives living. These same relatives he deliberately slights by leaving them a quantity of barley not worth the trouble of coming to collect. The debt of £100 to Mr. Fletcher is, I feel sure, connected with the cost of building the house. Note that the will is witnessed by no worthy neighbours, only by one old crony, by the writer and by two servants. Note the extraordinary generosity of his bequests to his daughter Katherine, and interpret it how you will. Note that he makes executors two boys, aged 13 and 15 respectively, yet entrusts their guardianship to his two brothers, for the handsome reward of £1 each. Note the revocation of all other wills, an unusual feature for this period. Note the reference to the household stuff which he "ought to injoye". And finally, note that there is no reference whatever to his wife! The obvious inference would seem to be that she was dead. But she was not dead! She was alive, and living in this house, or in one not far away. I have come across a will in which the husband cuts off his wife with the proverbial shilling. This is the only will I have ever seen in which a husband ignores completely the existence of his wife. The mystery deepens when one examines the probate certificate attached to the will. Beside it there is appended a note dated Feb. 6th 1588, declaring that Nicholas Campion, son of Thomas, now of age, "voluntarily and expressly renounced and refused to undertake the burden and execution of the aforesaid will."

The extent and nature of the family quarrel which is hinted at in those facts will never be revealed. Like the other disputes which have occurred under this roof, and there were plenty, it is decently buried in time and distance.

CHAPTER VI
Nicholas Campion

Nicholas was fifteen years old when he was formally admitted, on July 23rd 1583, to his father's holding of "a messuage and an 18 acre ware and 7 acres dispersed in the fields of Foxton" under the guardianship of his uncle Nicholas. His inheritance of the Docwra property is not recorded – there was no court competent to record it, for the manor of Docwra's had, for the time being, ceased to exist.

The surviving written records of Nicholas Campion are plentiful and, for the most part, prosaic in the extreme. He duly attended the manor-court with great regularity, or was "essoined" (i.e. represented and formally excused) by his friend and neighbour Will Fuller. He twice served as constable, in 1594 and again in 1598. He scrupulously avoided infringement of the by-laws and annoyance of his neighbours. True, he allowed his hedge to overgrow the lane (now Caxton Lane) leading from the Green into Down Field, but that was an oversight which hardly justified the threat of a 30/- fine. Also, he and others were warned not to use the headlands "between Bradway and Hayditch" as a short cut for their cattle on the way to the meadows after Lady Day; a bit of routine administration. Only once did he fall foul of the Archdeacon's watch-dogs, when in 1609 he was "presented for carting uppon Hallowmas daye". This ban on labour on Sundays and holy days was one aspect of the Church's vain struggle to maintain its juridical power against total takeover by the State. Few indeed were the farmers who never transgressed in this respect, for the needs of husbandry were paramount, and the usual penalty was a small fine or an admonition. Nicholas seems never to have served as churchwarden, and was somewhat lax in the matter of having his children baptised. Had he been born half a century later he would, I feel sure, have been a leading spirit in the ranks of the "free thinkers". It is quite clear that he was a very different type of man from his father.

He lived in this house with his mother and his brother William until the latter in 1594 married and took the house on the other side of the Green. Nicholas himself married in about 1596, when he was 28. Early marriages were not the rule in those days, unless, as often happened despite the archdiaconal vigilance and censure, there was a compulsory element. Nicholas and Alice had eight children, all born in this house:

1597	Samuel	– about whom more later.
1598	Mary	– who married Thomas Campion of London.
1600	Elizabeth	– who married Nathaniel Wright in 1628.
1603	William	– died four years later.
1606	Nathaniel	– died in less than a year.
1608	Nicholas	– survived his father.
1611	Anne	– survived her father.
1615	Nathaniel	– died at the age of 20.

The death of two children in infancy, out of a total of eight, was such a normal occurrence as to call for no comment. The fact that the two eldest girls made

Fig. 7 Interior of the cottage c.1600.

marriages of which their father disapproved, and that the youngest son also incurred his father's displeasure, adds some weight to my belief that Nicholas was a man of puritanical leanings. The presence of the grandmother in the house, until her death in 1617, may have caused some tension. Old Susan may have been partly to blame for the attitude adopted towards her by her late husband Thomas.

As a cottage historian, my chief interest in Nicholas Campion lies in the fact that it was he who "modernised" the house in the 1620s by the creation of the second "chamber" over the hall. In this he was in part following the fashion of the day, partly keeping up with the Fullers, Wells and Welbores, and partly doing what commonsense and necessity dictated. A growing family and an increasing amount of household "stuff", coupled with changing standards of home comfort, rendered three rooms wholly inadequate. And so that massive ceiling was inserted, new stairs constructed to give access to the new chamber (and to the old one), and a new window made to provide some light in it. When engaged on repairs to the chimney-breast recently I found a sheep's jaw-bone and a child's shoe set into the plaster of the chamber wall. I do not suppose for one moment that Nicholas believed in magic or witchcraft, but old traditions die hard! I regret that he did not see fit to carve a date on one of the beams. I regret even more my failure to locate a document whose existence is testified by a reliable witness, namely a brief statement of accounts for timber, straw etc., totalling about £25, to the best of my informant's memory, and said to have been found in the house. It could only have related to this work which Nicholas had done. Anyway, every bit of his handiwork is still there, so he certainly got his money's worth. I shudder to think what all those cubic feet of oak – at least twice as much as was really necessary – would cost today!

Nicholas could afford it all right. He owned three houses and about seventy acres of land, which was three times the average holding. By an odd chance, a detailed description of his Docwra holdings has survived, hidden amongst the Woodham papers. It is a copy, made in the mid-eighteenth century, of a terrier made in 1603 (according to the copier, but actually it must be later than that, probably 1633). Here it is, much abbreviated:

A terror or Boundari of Lande in Foxton, Houlden of Fee Mannor of Dockwais both free and Coppy wth the Annual Rentes thereout Issuing made – Nycholas & Samuell Campions Free Lande.

Downe Feilde.

	3r.	J. Fuller W., E. Rayner E., W head abut. on the Brooke against Conegrey.
1a.		on the Hill. J. Chase, W., Will – on E.
	1r.	same shott. Colledg land W., S head abut. upon hill.
1a.	2r.	T. Wells both sides. N head abut. on hill. S head on Berry Lands.
	1r.	next a balke S. Will Brock N. Colledg land W.
	1r.	lieth by the hill. J. Chase S. S head abut. Berry Lands.
	1r.	J. Chase S. W head uppon the Brooke.
1a.	2r.	T. Wells N. widow Barnes S. Abut. W on Brooke.
1a.		in longe Wadd. J. Fuller N. T. Wells S. abut. E on Woodway.
1a.	2r.	headland on hill. T. Bater W. S head abut. on Mortimers.

Fig. 8 Campion's house. c.1600.

	2r.	Will Wells E. abut S on Berrie lands.
—		
8a.	2r.	Totall of Lande in Downe feilde.
		Hamm Feilde.
1a.		at Coppett between to Baulks. E head abut. on the way leading to Barrington.
	2r.	same shott between Baulks, abut. as before.
	1r.	Ed. Nycholson N. a balk S. abut. E on Berryland.
1a.		a balk W. Berry land E. S head abut. on Mortimers land.
—		
2a.	3r.	Totall of land in Hamm Feilde.
		Hayditch Feilde.
2a.	2r.	at Hofferd. Berry land N. G. Wells S. W head abut. on way to Hofforde.
1a.		in Carle Croft Shott between balks. N head abut. Berrie lands.
1a.		same shott. J. Chase & T. Wells on N.
	2r.	in towne meadow Shott. W. Cock S. Barret on N.
	1r.	neare Broadway. J. Chase E. T. Wells N.
	2r.	in Bourne land. W. Brock S. G. Maris N.
	1½r.	R. Coulman W. Everet E. Abut. on several closes of J. Welbore on S. and on Cambridge Way on N.
	1r.	E. Rayner S. R. Coulman N. E head abut. on Way leading to Barrington.
	2r.	T. Wells sen. both sides. N head abut. T. Wells.
1a.		W. Fuller E. N head abut. on Berry lande.
1a.	2r.	headlands to Potter's Balke. W. Wells E. abut. S on Mortimers.
—		
9a.	3½r.	Totall in Hayditchfeild.
		Chadwell Feilde.
	2r.	W. Hyx N. the parsonage land S.
1a.		between balks. T. Wells S. J. Welbore N. abut. W on Mortimers.
	1r.	T. Barrett W. widow Garner E. S head on Draymore Way.
1a.		T. Starke N. R. Fuller S. W head on Pyrlpal Way.
	2r.	butting on said way. J. Fuller N. Mortimers on E head.
	2r.	J. Fuller S. T. Clarke N. W head on Pyrlpal Way.
	½r.	W. Wells W. a great balke E. S head on London Way.
2a.		at Rowditch between 2 greate balkes. E head on Newton Field.
1a.		at Bankshott. E. Rayner E. N. Singleton W. S head abut. uppon the Banke.
1a.		T. Willcocks S. J. Welbore N. J. Fuller on E head.
	2r.	W. Hyx N. J. Fuller S. E head on Woodway.
	2r.	T. Maris N. J. Fuller S. E head on Draymore Way.
1a.		T. Wells N. W. Wells S. E head on Draymore Way.
	2r.	Colledge land W. R. Fuller E. S head on Eastleys.

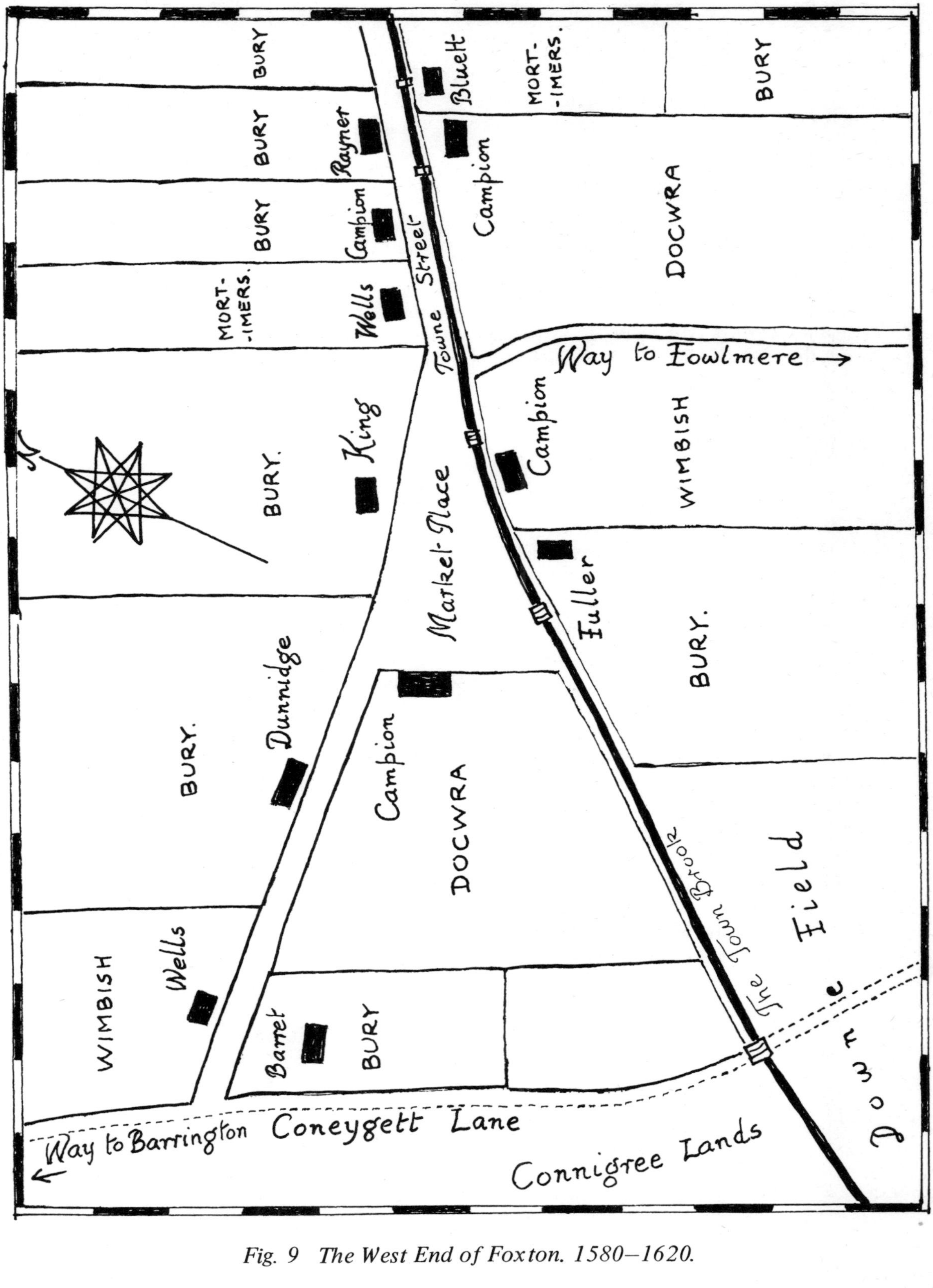

Fig. 9 The West End of Foxton. 1580–1620.

———

10a. 2r. Totall in Chadwell Field.

Meadow as followeth

3r. lying at Barrington Bridge. Mortimer land E. N head uppon the River.

1a. 2r. next the towne Meadows S. J. Chase N. E end abut. on the River in Hamm.

Feedings common at Lammas & when Chadwell Feild is in fallow

3a. at Chadwell. W. Wells N. Common Way to Chadwell S. E. end abut. uppon Chadwell springes of Water. W head on Maris lande arable.

One Messuage with a close of pasture thereunto adjoining, conteyning by estimacion 3ac. lying between the tenement of John Blewitt on the east syde and a comon lane leadinge to Jacklin's balke on the west side, the N head abutteth upon the Brooke & the S head abut. upon Downefeilde.

Total	arable	31 a.	2½r.		
	meadowe	2	1	39 ac.	3½r.
	feedings	3			
	pasture severall		3a.		

The yearly rent payable out of aforesaid lands due at Michaelmas to Manor of Dockwra's in Foxton 10s.
Memo. All the arable, meadow & feedings are conveyed to one C ——— for which he & heirs pay yearly rente of 6/8.
Item. Samuel still keepeth the Home Stall & the 3ac. several pasture for which his yearly portion of rent due to the ———— and is agreed to be 3/4.

The main object of reciting all that is to convey some idea of the practical problems created for the farmer by the Open-field system. Forty acres of land (by the way, the total given above is wrong – totals of land measurements nearly always were) in 45 pieces scattered all over the parish! To get from the meadow at Barrington Bridge to the acre next Chadwell Bank meant a journey of 2½ miles. How many miles were travelled, how many hours were spent in travelling in the course of a year in getting all those strips cultivated and harvested, no one knows. Why they tolerated such a system for close on a thousand years, no one knows. The even odder thing is that, so far as I know, nobody ever cultivated the wrong strip by mistake. With no map or plan to guide them, and nothing but the most rudimentary boundary marks, the farmers not only knew exactly the location and shape of their own strips, but those of most other farmers in the parish as well. One wonders if they ever thought or talked of anything else. It was all in their heads. They could not write it down because, with very rare exceptions, they could not read or write.

Another interesting feature of the above "terror", which must have been made for a specific reason, is that Nicholas's land was all leased to "one C ——" for a period of years. The reason for the lease is not far to seek. It appears in his will, dated 1634, here summarised:

"I, Nicholas Campion of Foxton, yeoman – sicke in body – to Alice my loveing

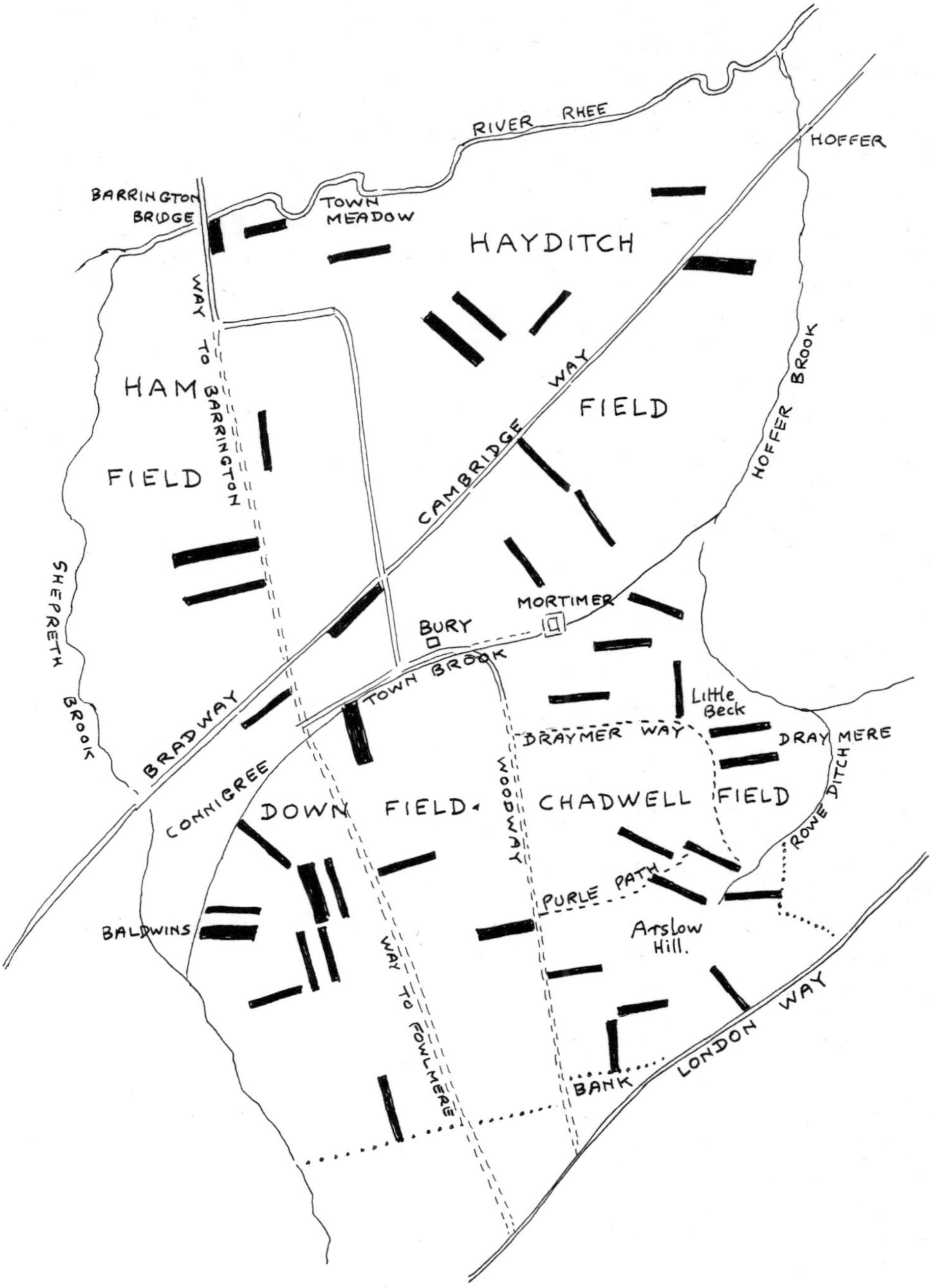

Fig. 10 Map showing how Campion's 40 acres were scattered in strips all over the parish.

wife £10 annually for the term of her natural life, to have sufficient meate and drinke, lodgeing and washeing in the house I now live in, with a conveniente chamber — to Alice my wife ii chestes with all the lininge, wollinge, brasse & peuter which is mine in the house — my will is that John Campion shall have meate, drinke & clotheing for his maintenance & IIs. to be paid him yearlie during his naturall life — to Marie my daugher, wife of Thomas Campion of London xiid. — to Elizabeth my daughter, wife of Nathaniell Write of Wimbish, Essex, xiid. — to Nathaniell Campion my sonne xiid. — to Nicholas Campion my sonne £50 to be paid within 3 yeres if he shal soe long live — to Ann Campion my daughter £50 to be paid within four yeres — to Catherine Tubbs my sister v s. — to the poore people of Foxton x s. — I do ordeine & make Samuel Campion my sonne sole executor — to pay my legacies and debts — and in consideration thereof I give Samuell my sonne all my goods & chattels which are ungiven."

Nicholas had in fact been very ill for some time before he died. Another chance discovery throws some light, all too little, on his illness; it is a single sheet of paper found amongst the archdiaconal documents in the University Library.

Spent in Nicholas Campion his sicknesse.

The proving his will & charges about the same one waye & other		0	14	0
To the minister for burying the descesed & for a sermon & for a mortuary		1	1	0
Tho Wells	Daniel Smyth of Barly	17	10	0
Oliver Ayler				
Tho Pentlow	Tho Pentlow	8	13	4
Mr. Sedgwick	To Alexander East	10	4	0
Mr. Sedgwick	To Jhno Sedgwick	10	8	0
Christian - - - - - -	Fisher East	5	4	0
Mathew Est	John Caudell Meldret	10	8	0
Raph Russell - - - - -	Henry Dentry of Meldreth	10	16	0
Allen's wyfe				
Mathew East	Joan Gatward of Royston	21	12	0
Mathew Est	Huggens of Barrington	86	8	0
	Robert Daye of Foxton	3	0	0
	Sum		3	4

The arithmetic was a bit too much for whoever compiled that list; his handwriting in places was a bit too much for me! The total actually comes to £185. 18. 4. Many of those items are obviously for medicines and doctor's fees. The only name known to me is that of Matthew East, the village writer, who had married Elizabeth Campion, widow of Nicholas's brother William who had died in 1603. It looks very much as though Samuel Campion stayed out of the picture and left others to settle his father's affairs. He was soon back in the picture.

CHAPTER VII
Samuel Campion

Samuel was born here, and spent his boyhood in and around this house. His schooling took place in the fields and woods, beside the brooks, amongst the sheep and horses; perhaps a little at his mother's knee, certainly sometimes across his father's; perhaps a little at the hands of Mr. Henry Brampton, vicar, or Mr. John Gibson, curate. Matthew East almost certainly taught him to write. Whoever claims the credit for it, Samuel was the first of the Campions able to write his name. In 1622 he married Hannah Greenwood, and they lived in the house where the Black Boy stood later. Five of their children were born there, the rest in this house. Here is the full score:

1623	Alice	–	married John Chapman.
1625	Sara	–	married William Dods.
1628	Mary	–	married John Westrop.
1631	Samuel	–	(?)
1633	Hannah	–	married Thomas Bigsby.
1636	Elizabeth	–	died five years later.
1638	Nathaniel	–	died at the age of 15.
1641	Elizabeth	–	survived her father.
1645	Susan	–	survived her father.

Apart from those facts, the life of Samuel is in many ways obscure. And those "facts" are not at all clear. I have, for instance, no record of the death of young Samuel. And Elizabeth, the second Elizabeth, presents a problem. She was undoubtedly alive when old Samuel died in 1679, and yet "Elizabeth Campion, daughter of Samuel" died in 1676. Did young Samuel die young, or did he marry against his father's wishes, and was he utterly cast out therefor? It could well be. Indeed, when we come to look at old Samuel's will, it will be evident that *all* his children who married did so without their father's blessing. What sort of a father can he have been? And to what extent was he himself responsible for the ill-fortune and unhappiness which marked his life? Was it something inherited from his grandfather?

He had a bad start as head of the family by inheriting the pile of debts which we saw in the last chapter. No doubt it was partly that which compelled him to sell the house opposite the Black Boy. It was bought by John Welbore. Samuel never appears as a tenant of the Bury manor. John Welbore also bought the house where Samuel had begun his married life.

The real curse of Samuel's life was all those girls. Nine children, and seven of them girls! How could a man run a farm without sons? Girls might be all right for hay-making, milking, feeding the calves, looking after the hens, picking saffron (better than boys for that), tying sheaves at harvest. Oh yes, girls had their uses. But for ploughing, mowing, carting, ditching, hedging, threshing – strong arms were needed. Strong arms were lacking. There was only one answer – sheep.

As it happened, Samuel's being driven to sheep-farming coincided with a return of sheep to fashion and favour. The last big sheep boom had been a hundred and fifty years before, when it had resulted in large-scale enclosure and disappearing villages in many areas, and magnificent churches and manor-houses in others. The present boom was on nothing like that scale, and was of much shorter duration. Still, Samuel went in for sheep in a big way, by his standards. His sole appearance in the manor-court rolls, in 1649, is this:

"200 sheep belonging to the lands called Connigree Lands in the occupation of John Welbore, gent. and Samuel Campion, ought to be kept in a separate fold."

Sheep on the commons, especially other tenants' sheep on the commons of the Bury, were a nuisance.

"No sheep to be in the common fields from 25 March until after harvest. No sheep to be pastured in the meadows from Bury Piece to Hoffer, nor in any of the Sheard pastures."

Feeding was getting scarcer every year, and this was not good sheep country in any case. Samuel's luck was definitely out.

Then there was that awful business of the church. Enough to drive any man to the devil, that was! When Samuel's great-grandfather was a boy, everybody was Catholic, and nobody thought of being anything else. In his grandfather's day, everybody in Foxton was Protestant, and it didn't seem to make much difference. Then in his father's time, there came Puritans, and Samuel couldn't understand what that meant, though his father nearly was one. Now there was talk of a return to the old style of religion. Bishop Matthew Wren of Ely was going to shake up the parishes of his diocese, discipline his parsons and churchwardens, secure a proper respect for morality, as understood by the Church, enforce devotion and bring his flock to heel. No more of this "liberty of conscience" nonsense.

As luck would have it – and luck, bad luck, always seemed to be lying in wait for him – Samuel had been talked into accepting the office of churchwarden, in the place of Edward Nicholson, by his friend and neighbour George Wells, just a few months before Bishop Wren made his "visitation" in 1638. Not that the Bishop actually came to Foxton. That would have been bad enough. What he did was far worse. He sent a questionnaire, 146 questions to be answered in writing, touching upon everything from the form of service to the morals, public and private, of the parishioners; the answers to be returned to the Consistory Court at Great St. Mary's Church, Cambridge. Samuel and George made their answers as brief and non-committal as possible, or left them blank, maintaining a discreet silence on the morals of their neighbours. Moreover, they declined to attend the Court, where further questions might be asked, and in consequence were suspended from duty. The vicar, Mr. Vaughan, likewise got a rocket. They could not get away with this dodging, and were forced to get the churchyard fence repaired, to alter the reading-desk so that the minister "looked northward", and to "exhibit a terrier" of church lands.

The pendulum soon swung the other way. The tide of Puritanism was rising fast, sweeping away everything "root and branch". Popery, and anything savouring of popery, was to be abolished for ever. This included images, crucifixes, inscriptions, altar-rails – the lot. People henceforth should worship in plain white-washed buildings furnished with a font, a pulpit, seats and a communion-table. William

Dowsing, Commissioner appointed to supervise the cleansing of East Anglia, sent his agents to Foxton church, and reported on March 13th 1644

"we brake 60 popish Superstitious Pictures and gave order to brake down & take down 2 crosses."

The church interior for the next thirty years remained a wreck, a shambles. Not that it mattered to Samuel Campion. He never went near the place again, until he was carried there. Two of his daughters were excommunicated when Bishop Wren returned at the Restoration. Who cared? By that time over two-thirds of the villagers were either Dissenters or nothing.

The Campion star was declining fast. Samuel lived on with his loyal wife and two unmarried daughters, both now well past marriageable age, and not much of a match anyway, for their dowry was dwindling at equal pace with the decline of such charms as they ever had. Their brother-in-law took pity on their plight and left them £5 apiece in his will. Samuel clearly must have let the land to a tenant during his later years; he could not farm it, for he was getting on for eighty. He might have coped with a few sheep, but no more than that. He died in 1679. His will is the will of an impoverished, unhappy, penitent old man.

"In the name of God, Amen. I, Samuel Campion of Foxton in the County of Cambridge, although in weakness of body yet, thanks be to God, in perfect soule and memory, do declare and make this my last will and testament in the manner and form following: first, being penitent and sorrowful from the bottome of my heart for all my sins past, and do trust and believe by the merits of Jesus Christ assuredly to be saved and commit my body to the earth and my Soul to God that gave it; and as touching my Messuage, Houses and Lands & tenements I give unto Hanna my wife to have and to hold the same to her and to her assigns for ever during the term of her natural (life) and after her decease I give and bequeath the same unto my two maiden daughters Elizabeth and Susan their heirs and assigns for ever; item I give unto Hanna the wife of Thomas Bigby one shilling, to Sara the wife of William Dods one shilling, to Mary the wife of John Westrop one shilling, and to John Chapman my son-in-law one shilling; and all the rest of my goods and chattells I give and bequeath to Hanna my wife and do nominate and appoint her sole executrix of this my last will and testament. In witness whereof I have hereto put my hand and seale the 23rd day of July in the year of our Lord 1679."

He goes far beyond the standard formula in his expression of piety and penitence. But however penitent he may be, he has no intention of forgiving those errant daughters, or of forgoing the time-honoured method of showing his disapproval. For he was not so poor that he could not afford more than a shilling apiece. No, his last defiant gesture was to cut them all off with a shilling. And we still do not know – we never shall know – just what it was that made him hate his daughters. Unless it was that he never forgave them for being daughters! A strange man, indeed!

He was "buried in woollen" in accordance with the Act of Parliament which prescribed it (a series of Acts, in fact, from 1666 onwards, intended to aid the cloth-manufacturing industry). Susan Campion and Mary Adleson signed the affidavit before William Layer, Esq., J.P. (son of the historian John Layer).

Faithful old Hannah followed him to the grave less than a year later. She too was buried in woollen, and only Mary Adleson signed the affidavit. No mention of Susan or Elizabeth. It looks very much as though they were not at their mother's funeral. They disappear from the scene. Evidently the house, and such land as was left, was sold to John Welbore, if it had not already been sold to his father Philip Welbore. The house was not to be owner-occupied again for another two hundred and fifty years.

CHAPTER VIII
Welbores

With the Welbores – Wildbores originally, then modified by gentility, finally reverting to its original rough form under the corrupting influence of the nineteenth century – we move up the social scale a rung or two. They belonged to the layer of society whose members, in their own and the general estimation, were entitled to the label of "Gent." or "Esq." There were four generations of them connected with Foxton, just as there were four generations of St. Georges and four of Campions. The first of them, Philip, only concerns us in that he bought part of the Docwra estate when Thomas Campion bought the rest. He also bought the Bury lands which had belonged to the St. Georges, later to the Burgoyne family, and built for himself a handsome house in the centre of the village, where the University Tutorial Press now stands. He owned property in Thriplow, Elmdon, Heydon and Chrishall, and was a very wealthy man. His three daughters, well endowed, made good marriages, and his three sons were well provided for. The eldest, John, born in 1588, inherited the house and the Foxton lands. Philip is the only one of the persons named in my chronicle whose memory has been perpetuated, on a neat marble slab in the church:

Philip Welbore he was here interred,
He served God and the Poore relieved:
We knowe he is not lost but sent before,
His friends all left, his absence to deplore.
Nor can his Virtues ever be forgott,
Thoughe in this Grave his Corpes be dead and rot.
the 12 of March he made a Godlye End,
Anno one thousand six hundred & fiveteene.

Everything known about him suggests that he was indeed a gentleman, not just a "Gent." He deserved a better poet to write his epitaph.

John Welbore continued the tradition of his father. He enlarged the estate by purchase of more Docwra land, which he himself farmed, and like Samuel Campion, but for a different reason, he went in for sheep-farming. He married Ann Wentworth in 1620, and they had five children, of whom three girls died in infancy. He played his due part in the affairs of the village, without however filling that ever-present void, the need for a strong, benevolent figure to serve as a natural leader. He died in 1661 at the ripe age of 73. I quote from his will only those items which I find interesting in themselves, or which have a bearing on my story, and one which gives a hint of trouble to come:

> "I give to William Ayloffe my grandchild £100 when he reaches 21 years, to be paid in the porch of the parish church of Foxton – I give to Sir Thomas Wendy and my Lady Wendy 20/- apiece to buy both a ring – I give to William Layer of Shepreth 20/- to buy him a ring – I give to Mrs. Elizabeth Oxford of Foxton, widow, dwelling in the house she dwells in with the other Roomes & houses in her occupation for six years from the Feast of St. Thomas next if she live so long,

she paying one penny, and keeping the houses in repair, provided if my son Philip shall see fit to remove her out of the said house and houses any time within six years, he shall pay her at the rate of 40 shillings aydand from the time of her removal until six years be expired — I give to Wendy Oxford and Philip Oxford £3. 6. 8. apiece towards their being put out as Apprentice — I give to Charles Baron my ancient Servant £5 — unto Nathaniell my Housekeeper 6/8 — to Anna Bentham my ancient Cooksmaid 40/- — to Susanna Hawkes my dayry maid 10/- — I give to the poor of Foxton £4 — All the rest — to Philip Welbore."

Wendy Oxford, by the way, was a boy, not a girl! It would be tempting to digress here and say something about the illustrious Wendy family, also to speculate as to how their name came to be used as a forename in the Oxford family, but I must resist the temptation.

Young Philip was not of the same calibre as his father or grandfather. Perhaps his father had treated him too well; Fate was to restore the balance, tip it too far the other way, in fact. Things went well for a time. He was 23 when he inherited his father's wealth and position. A year later he married Susan Bambridge and settled down as a family man. In 1664 his first son John was born, followed by Philip a year later. The next year a third son, Thomas, was born, and died a few days later. The next year, 1667, a daughter, Mary, came into the world only to leave it almost at once, taking her mother with her. Such a blow would shake the strongest of men, which Philip Welbore was not. Those two little boys obviously needed a mother, and Philip needed a wife. Within two years he had found one, and soon had another daughter. But he seems to have married trouble. Who was to blame, Philip or his wife, no one can now say. Clearly Philip blamed his wife; her side of the story is not known, but she had plenty with which to reproach him. Reading between the lines, or indeed just reading the lines, of his will, one can see a story of dissension at home (when he was at home), neglect of the estate, gambling, spending, debts and more debts. If ever a man can be said to have "gone to pieces", that man is Philip Welbore. Practically the whole estate — which may have included this cottage; I rather think it did — was mortgaged. He died in 1675 at the age of 37, ruined in every sense of the word. His will is of enormous length and verbosity; I quote here only a few extracts. All his land was to be sold to pay his debts

"except for the debt which William Le Neeve claymeth or pretendeth to claym of me secured unto him by lands in Foxton late Joseph Greenwood, deceased, and formerly Samuel Campion's."

He left his wife an annuity out of the proceeds of the sale:

"£200 for the maintenance of herselfe and Elizabeth my daughter — Provided that my wife shall relinquish — all her right and title of Dower — And if my wife shall refuse to do so, then I give the said £200 to my two sons John and Philip to be equally divided."

His son Philip was to have an annuity of £20 from the Foxton lands, and John to have the house.

"I commit the guardianship and education of my two sons unto the care and government of my worthy cousin Christopher Bambridge, B.D., late Fellow of Christ's College in Cambridge."

"I give to my sister Mrs. Susannah Ayloffe, widow, all the wearing apparrell of my former wife which is now in my dwelling-house in Foxton."

Could it have been this matter of clothes, I wonder, which began all the trouble? Greater tragedies have sprung from more trivial causes.

Philip Welbore, however, had had more friends than he thought, perhaps more than he deserved. Foremost amongst them was the worthy Dr. Bambridge, his "cousin" (actually he must have been father-in-law or brother-in-law). It would be he who sent the two boys to Huntingdon Grammar School. It was he, too, with Robert Baron of Shelford and William Layer of Shepreth, who rescued the Welbore estate, which was not sold after all. Indeed it was enlarged by the purchase of the rest of the Docwra estate (definitely including this cottage by now) when Samuel Campion died. The boys did well at school, especially John, who at 16½ was admitted as a pensioner at Trinity College, where he matriculated in 1682. Three years later he became a Scholar, and took his degree in 1686. Philip was admitted as a sizar at Christ's College in 1685 and took a degree in Medicine in 1688. John was admitted to the Middle Temple in 1687, and his legal career began. No farming for him, and no "country gentleman" nonsense either! He had already learnt, or was soon to discover, that there was more money to be made by drafting those indentures relating to the sale and lease of estates than there was from the farming of the estates themselves. In 1694 he was called to the Bar, and his time was largely taken up with his affairs in London. He still found time, however, to manage his estate in the country, which, almost as a matter of course, grew steadily larger. He bought half of the Bury manor. He acted as Steward of Mortimer's manor. He revived the title of "Manor of Docwra's" (he spelt it "Dockwray's") – thereby earning my gratitude, for had he not done so the title would certainly have disappeared, and my house would not have been "called Docwra's" in 1830. He would have earned even more of my gratitude if he had taken steps to preserve the many historical documents which came into his hands or to which he had access.

He never married. Perhaps subconscious memories of his father's unhappy experience were to blame for that; perhaps he was wedded to his profession. His legal career was crowned in 1720 by appointment to the King's Bench. He ought to have been a very rich man; he ought to have been a very happy man. He was neither. In 1724 he leased "for one peppercorn if it shall be demanded" most of his estate to Samuel Herring, Citizen and Merchant Taylor of London. Such a lease was the preliminary to an outright sale. But the sale did not take place. John Welbore, having lived largely by managing other people's affairs, in the end bungled his own affairs. He died in 1727, alone but for his housekeeper, in the house which his great-grandfather had built, surrounded by his "common plaie or plead Book and other my Manuscripts of the Law which I have wrote with my own hands."

His will gives a detailed description of the estate, including "all that my mannor of Dockwrai's". For a lawyer's will, though, it must surely be unique; it bears no date, names no legatee, and has no witnesses! His former legal colleagues managed to get round such trifling difficulties, and Samuel Herring became the owner of the Welbore estate.

For the next hundred years the Welbore estate, as it continued to be called, included this cottage, ownership of which can be quickly related. From Herring it passed to John Seddon, who lived in the Welbore house, married a Hurrell, and was buried in Foxton church in 1758. His brother Richard Seddon inherited, left it to his nephew Richard Seddon, who sold it in 1774 to Thomas Parker, from whom it passed by purchase to Bendysh.

Let us return to 1679 – and the Rayners.

Fig. 11 Rayner's house. c.1700.

CHAPTER IX
Rayners

Yes, the Rayners. Few families can ever have been more appropriately named. They did not merely "rain", they poured, and went on for ever – almost. There were Rayners in Foxton in the early 13th century; they were absent for a time, to return again at the beginning of the 14th century, from which time they were on the scene for 550 years. By all the laws of genetics, if there are any, they ought to have died out somewhere around the year 1600. In actual fact they chose that very time, in defiance of plague, pestilence and infant mortality, to begin the performance of a feat which must surely constitute a record in human proliferation. Between 1609 and 1809 there were 121 Rayners born in this one small parish alone, to say nothing of adjacent parishes, and plus a good number whose baptism, if it took place, was not recorded. In the same period 97 Rayners were buried in Foxton. In 1680 there were 14 male Rayners in Foxton either married or soon to marry, and five of them were called Edward Rayner. It would be surprising if Rayners had not occupied this house. There can be few old houses in the village which were not occupied by Rayners at some time or other. And indeed they did live here – six generations of them, spanning 144 years.

The first of them was "Edward Rayner the Younger", son of Edward. He moved in with his family when the Campions moved out. He and his wife Sara had seven children, five of them born here:

1676	William.	
1678	Sara.)	
	Robert.)	
	Edward.)	Baptisms not recorded, but all alive at father's death.
	Mary.)	
	Ellen.)	
	Elizabeth.)	

Edward was clearly a man of some substance, a hard worker and a real farmer. He built up the holding once more to a viable farm of about fifty acres, still scattered all over the parish, of course. He was not rich, not to be compared with the Welbores, but he had all he needed for the sustenance of his family; and what he had was earned by the sweat of his brow and the labour of his hands – and the hands of his wife and children! He died in November, 1694, at the age of 57 – fifty-seven years of work, day in, day out, seven days a week! Was it worth it? There is no hint of dissatisfaction in his will; there is rather a hint of pride in a lifetime of useful achievement:

"I bequeath to Sara Rayner my wife that house and grounds I now live in, and after her death to William Rayner my son – to Sara Rayner my 5 acres of free land late Chase's – to William Rayner 12 acres of free land late Campion's – to William Rayner a close of pasture, late Oliver's, provided that William pay to my daughter Sara £20 when she shall reach the age of 21, failing which Sara shall have the close of pasture – to Robert my son an 18 acre ware land late

Welbore's – to Edward my son 9 acres, late Misson's, and 4 acres of arable, late Sarah Rayner my aunt, and one small close of pasture with an orchard and a little cottage late Standlands – to my three daughters Mary, Ellen and Elizabeth, £50 to be equally divided between them and paid when they reach the age of 21 years – to Sara my wife the rest of my goods and movables."

When Edward died, an inventory was made of all his possessions, in and about the house, in accordance with the law, and as a precaution against fraudulent dealing. The value of such documents in revealing the structure and contents of houses of the period is obvious. Here it is:

Foxton Nov. 6th 1694.

A trew Inventory of all the goods and Chattells of Edward Raynor the younger, yeomen, late deceased.

Imprimis his wearing apparrell and money in his purse		3	6	8.
Item.	In the Parlour one jone bedstead, one press, one lenen cubard, four chayers, one fether bed, one bowster, two peulews, one coverlett, two blankates, with other small things	5	13	4.
Item.	In the hall one jone table and six jone stoules, one press, one littell table with other small lumber	2	19	6.
Item.	In the kitchen the bruen vesseles, the bras and Pewter with other small lumber	4	6	8.
Item.	In the Parlor Chamber two littel bedsteads, one fether bed, one coverlet, two blankets, one bouster, four cheastes	4	1	4.
Item.	In the Hall Chamber two trunkes and a tabell		13	4.
Item.	In Linning	8	6	8.
Item.	Corne in the Barne of Corne	48	5	4.
Item.	In the yard three horses, three cows, three hogges	20	5	2.
Item.	Two Carts, plows, harros and geres	6	6	8.
Item.	In the feld eight acres of wheat and Ray	12	5	6.
Item.	In tilth and Brockland to sow	21	4	4.
Item.	In Safrongrounde one roode and halfe	6	6	8.
Item.	In Safronn in the hous	3	3	4.
Item.	In foules in the yard		10	0.
	Sum. tot.	147	14	6.

Prised by us

Nathaniel Singleton senr.
Edward Rayner made his mark
Robert Taylor

Sara relict et exect. 17th Nov. 1694.

(Note: surprisingly few explanations are needed in the above. "jone" is "joined", i.e. made by a joiner; "peulews" are "pillows"; "press" is a sort of wooden box; "geres" means harness: "tilth" was land ploughed in the spring and left fallow all summer; "brockland" was land ploughed in the autumn, needing to be "broken" for an autumn sowing.)

Bless you, Nathaniel, Edward and Robert! That is the only really detailed picture of this house in all its long history. It converts so many speculations into certainties, bringing back the past over a span of nearly three centuries! One can see those four girls trooping up the stairs to their two 'littel' beds, taking out their best clothes on Sundays, each from her own 'cheaste', or seated at meal-times each on her own stool, each with her pewter bowl and plate. One can see those piles of linen spread out on the hedge to dry in the sun before being stowed away in the chests and presses. One can smell the ale 'bruen' in the kitchen, the saffron in the chamber over the hall, where now no one slept. From the yard comes the thud and jingle of horses returning to the stable, the squeal of pigs waiting to be fed, the lowing of cows waiting to be milked. Harvest is over, and all the threshing done. The autumn sowing of wheat and rye has been started, the rest of the seed is waiting to go in. What a blessing to have three sturdy sons!

Sara, then, continued to live in this house, with her sons farming the land, William, who was eighteen when his father died, soon decided to leave the overcrowded nest and set up home on his own; he married Anne, and they lived in the house opposite the Black Boy. He died in 1736.

To have several sons was a distinct blessing for a father whilst he was alive, but it was a circumstance which contained a built-in guarantee of gradual impoverishment. For when the father died, his estate was divided into several smaller estates. This meant that each son had to start from scratch and build up his substance as his father had done. From the point of view of morality and character-building, this was no doubt an excellent thing. But from an economic viewpoint it was disastrous, especially when economic conditions were changing as they were throughout the eighteenth century. By the middle of the century it was still possible for a man and his family to live on about twenty acres; it was absolutely impossible for him to make the surplus money needed to purchase extra land, the value of which rose steadily. Whatever land came on to the market was snapped up by men, such as the Hurrells, who already had a large amount of land and capital. The Hurrells grew steadily richer; the Rayners, by virtue of their proliferation, grew steadily poorer. I'm sure that there is a lesson in this for the economist, the politician and the social historian, but I cannot see any remedy.

It might be apposite here to give some sort of picture of that proliferation, even though few of these Rayners directly enter into my story. Here is a list of the Rayners and their offspring during the 18th century. The date given in each case is the date of birth of the first child. An asterisk denotes a child known to have died in infancy:

James & Susan	1695	Susan, Sara, Elizabeth, Dorothy, Moulton.
Edward & Sara	1696	John*, William.
William & Anne	1713	Edward, William.
Matthew & Martha	1716	Anne, William.
Robert & Elizabeth	1720	William.
John & Elizabeth	1721	James, Sarah, Elizabeth, Susan, Dorothy*.
Robert & Sarah	1725	Sarah.
Edward & Elizabeth	1726	Edward, William*, William, Sarah, John*, Elizabeth*, Mary*.

Fig. 12 One Rayner escapes oblivion.

Fig. 13 The saffron crocus. Cultivated here from c.1500–c.1740.

William & Elizabeth	1728	William, Edward*, Francis*, Hellen, Elizabeth, Edward.
James & Ann	1734	Numon.
John & Catherine	1736	Dorothy*, Bransome*.
Robert & Mary	1736	William, Robert.
William & Anne	1737	Anne*, William.
Thomas & Mary	1738	Thomas, John, William, James*, Susan, Edward*, Elizabeth.
Edward & Elizabeth	1751	Edward, William, John*, John, James, Ellen.
John & Sara	1758	John, Susan.
William & Elizabeth	1758	William.
William & Mary	1761	Edward, Mary*, Ann, Thomas*.
William & Elizabeth	1771	Elizabeth*, William*, James*.
William & Ann	1772	William*, Elizabeth*, Mary, Anne, Robert, Thomas.
William & Elizabeth	1775	James, Edward, Thomas, Elizabeth.
William & Elizabeth	1792	William*, Susan, Sara, Ann*.

And that, let me remind you, is nothing compared with the Rayner crop during the 17th century, when families of eight, nine and ten were a commonplace!

It might well be wondered how anyone could keep track of the occupants of any one house through all that tangle of names. It would have been easier if one of the Rayner lads had married a Jane or Matilda occasionally, but it looks as though they had little choice — it had to be Sara, Mary, Ann or Elizabeth. However, by working backward, and by elimination, and by deduction, it was possible. I'm afraid that, after all the labour and ingenuity, there is very little to tell.

When William departed, his brother Edward was left to carry on here, with his wife Sara and his old mother Sara, who lived on until 1724, by which time she must have been over eighty. Edward left the house and land to his only son William, born in 1700, who married Ann. Their son William, born in 1741, married Ann, and had six children of whom two died in infancy. Robert was born in 1776. Thomas "enlisted for a soldier" and died in one of the London hospitals in 1798.

I know nothing about those Rayners apart from the fact that they were born, they got married, they had children, they died. How many millions of human beings are there, have there been, will there be, of whom that is all there is to know? They left no wills or inventories. They left no mark anywhere — some of them did in fact scratch their initials on the church walls; otherwise, oblivion. There may be a lesson here for the philosopher!

What I do know is that the status of the Rayners steadily declined, not because of anything they did or left undone, simply because of the change in social conditions which was taking place around them. Whilst a revolution in agriculture and economics was occurring, they, the Rayners, were stagnating. Not merely the Rayners, but dozens of other small farmers. One by one these small farmers dropped out of the race and became labourers. Better to work for William Hurrell, even at 9/- a week, than to go on paying rent and rates and try to make a living from their own ten or twenty acres. Most former yeomen's houses during this period became labourers' cottages, usually housing two families. This house, however, kept its status for a little longer. Robert Rayner was still calling himself "yeoman" in 1800. That fact alone may have contributed to the preservation of the house. There was no embellishment or addition made to it during the period other than the construction of a brick oven in the fireplace, in about 1770, I should think. But the house was cared for and kept in good repair, no doubt of that.

At the beginning of the 19th century the Land Tax Returns provide a new source of enlightenment. In 1811 Robert Rayner is shown as occupying property assessed at an annual value of £3 – this house with its yard and garden – and farming land owned by Mr. Elborne assessed at £6. In 1820 Robert Rayner and Mary are shown in occupation of house and garden only. Robert, still only 44 years old, had given up farming and become a labourer. Four years later, worn out by the unequal struggle, he died, leaving his sister Mary as the sole surviving Rayner of the tribe. She had inherited from another William Rayner the house next to the churchyard, where she lived on until 1847. The female of the species always outlived the male.

CHAPTER X
Enclosure – before and after

In this section of my chronicle a number of separate threads are drawn together. It deals with a period of complications involving many people of different interests, and tells something of an event which changed the face of the village and shaped the destiny of much of it. First the people: we take up the thread of manorial history where we left it dangling in Chapter VIII.

Thomas Parker, another gentleman-lawyer like John Welbore, after serving as Steward of the Bury manor, became its owner in 1772. The management of the estate had for over thirty years been very lax indeed; rents had been collected, of course, but scores of transfers of property had taken place without being registered at the "manor-court" (which by this time meant no more than a meeting attended by the Steward and his clerk and such tenants as cared to attend, which was very few) and that meant that the entry-fines had not been paid. Parker himself, as Steward, was too busy to rectify this state of affairs, but when he became Lord of the Manor, and in a position to employ two Stewards, he saw to it that they did their job, and did it far better than he had done it. Between 1772 and 1774 more than sixty property-transfers were registered and the books brought up-to-date. Parker continued his investment in land by purchasing, in 1775, all the former Welbore estate, including "that Manor of Dockways or Dockwrays or Dockrass in Foxton". (It wasn't that they did not know how to spell, or did not know the proper name; it was simply that, the more words you could put into a document, the higher the fee!)

This was an age of wild speculation, of rising values, of money-madness – the beginning of the crazy system which has since come to be regarded as an inevitable concomitant to modern civilisation. Having plunged deep, and found nothing but a swarm of other plungers, one had to plunge even deeper to get clear of the crowd – one hoped. To buy the Welbore estate, Parker borrowed from Robert Frisby, an "oilman". Having purchased it, Parker and Frizby promptly mortgaged it for £1000 to Messrs. Webley and Crump, two more London merchants. (The word "mortgage" is not used; technically they "leased the property for 500 years on payment of one peppercorn only if demanded.") Parker bought more land, including most of John Rayner's, and borrowed more money. In 1778 his debt had reached £1500. By 1782 it had increased by a further £1045. In 1786 it stood at a round £5000. You might well wonder what was being done with all this money, and with similar sums being spent by other "gentlemen". The answering of your question would provide material for a novel, several novels. Indeed it has. Go and look at the numerous country mansions of the period, set in their spacious parks (those which have not since been converted to air-fields and housing estates), or at the elegant town-houses set in sedate "squares" (many of them now converted to "flats"); do that, people them with characters from Fielding, Smollett, Fanny Burney and Thackeray, and you will soon come to understand what is meant, and what it cost, to be a "gentleman". As for this humble cottage and its few acres of land, I doubt whether Parker ever saw it, or gave a thought to it or its occupants. The few pounds which the latter contributed, after a year of sweat and toil, to pour into the financial drain of Thomas Parker's existence, might just as well have been thrown into any other drain. (Only there weren't any!)

Parker's problem was solved for him by Richard Bendysh, of Barrington. In 1787 Bendysh bought from Parker, Frisby, Crump "and others" the whole of the Foxton property for £7400 – mortgages, annuities and all. I wish you could see the document relating to the sale! Here is a small extract from it, by way of illustration of my foregoing remark about legal practices:

> " – together with all outhouses, buildings, barns, coach-houses, stables, erections, dovecotes, yards, gardens, orchards, tofts, crofts, lands, meadows, pastures, glebelands, heaths, moors, marshes, wastes, waste grounds, sheepwalks, folds, foldcourses, liberty of folding, feeding, warrens, commons, common of pasture, turbary, mines, minerals, quarries, multures, mills, customs, tolls, duties, furzes, timber, other trees, woods, underwoods, the ground and soil thereof, mounds, banks, headlands, foures, hedges, ditches, freeboards, tithes, ways, waters, watercourses, ponds, pools, fishings, fowlings, Courts Leet, Courts Baron and other Courts, perquisites and profits of Court, View of Frankpledge and all that to View of Frankpledge doth belong, reliefs, heriots, fines, sums of money, amerciaments, goods and chattels of felons, felons of themselves, fugitives and outlawed persons, deodands, waifs, strays, chief rents, quit rents, and other rents, boons, services, franchises, jurisdictions, privileges, easements, emoluments, hereditaments and appurtenances whatsoever."

They forgot to mention the market! Of course, it had not been in existence for the past 250 years. But some of those terms listed above had had no legal validity for the past 400 years! The whole paragraph could have been expressed in one half line. The amusing thing – amusing to me, at any rate – is that Thomas Parker, a lawyer, had to pay for it: as neat an example of "the biter bit" as I have ever seen.

With the name of Bendysh we come into contact with one of the oldest of English county families. Their history dates back to the 13th century, since when they had had their ancestral home at Barrington Hall. I have not the space to trace it here, and it does not really concern us, close as has always been the connection between the Bendyshes and Foxton, until 1787, when Richard Bendysh owned the manors of Foxton Bury with Wimbish & Chatteris, Mortimer's and Docwra's – the whole of Foxton, in fact, apart from what William Hurrell owned in his own right.

The Hurrell family likewise, though not of "county" status, has a distinguished history. The Foxton Hurrells were farmers first, with social status a very poor second. The only Hurrells who concern us were Williams. William the Elder was born in 1736 at the Bury, farmed there all his life, and steadily built up an estate of several hundred acres. His son, William the Younger, born in 1762, also at the Bury, inherited on his father's death in 1791 this estate, which he enlarged by successive purchases until, on the eve of the Enclosure, he owned six houses (including Foxton House then being built) and about 500 acres of land. In addition to those 500 acres he was farming another 500 acres which he rented from John Bendysh,

Esq., son of Richard. The majority of the men in Foxton, whose ancestors had been small yeoman farmers, were now labourers working for William Hurrell. This was just one aspect of the Agrarian Revolution.

Now a new name is introduced into the story – Elborne. Here again is a side-light on the social and economic history of the times. Until the 18th century, country land had belonged to country men, who lived on it and farmed it. Then townsmen discovered that land was a good investment for the money which they made in the towns. Land was the one commodity which lasted for ever. Money and all other commodities could be stolen, spent, lost, frittered away, depreciated, burnt, wasted – so could land, but, when any or all of those eventualities occurred, the land was still there. William Elbourn, baker, of Cambridge, began by buying a few acres from William Dunn, publican of the "Blackamoor's Head", in 1775. He and his son continued the practice of buying up a little bit at a time. In 1789 William Elbourne the Younger bought from William Wallis, another Cambridge baker, the house next to this (on the west) and a few more acres. In 1804 Elbourne bought from Robert Rayner

> "All those two Nine Acre Ware Lands in Foxton aforesaid containing by estimation Sixteen Acres and one Rood more or less holden of the said Manor by the yearly Rent of Nine Shillings."

Robert Rayner made his mark – a very shaky cross – and relinquished ownership of his land, though continuing to farm it. In 1814 William the Younger took surrender from James Pink of Foxton, carpenter, and Elizabeth his wife, "in Consideration of One hundred and ten Pounds of lawful Money of Great Britain", of the Messuage or Tenement Barn Orchard and Hereditaments opposite the Black Boy. (Just to show how inextricably are interwoven the threads of local history – of any history, for that matter – Elizabeth Pink was descended from the Oxfords whom we met in John Welbore's will, and the house in question was once the house of John Rayner, from whom our Robert Rayner was descended.)

Let us not misinterpret the action or motives of William Elbourne the Younger. The Pinks did not lose their home when Elbourne bought it. It was sold "subject nevertheless to the liberty and privilege of each of them living in the said premises rent free during their joint lives and the life of the survivor." The strange thing is – it seems strange to me now, knowing what was to happen in more recent times – that, with all this scramble for property going on, nobody was ever turned out of a house. When one of the cottages in Stocker's Lane was sold in 1832 (one of the six which later became my property), it was sold "subject to the life of a Female aged 74 years". Was this humanitarianism? Was it something to do with the Poor Laws, and the determination to prevent people from being made chargeable to the parish? Or was it just that houses did not matter so much as the land? Social historians, please note.

Then came the Enclosure. Initiated in 1826, at the instigation of William Hurrell and John Bendysh, it was completed on June 10th, 1830. All the common fields, the wastes, the shotts, strips, doles, baulks, rights of common etc. which had existed, unchanged except for a gradual extension, for nigh on a thousand years, were abolished. The land was re-allocated in compact blocks and pieces. No one owned any more or any less than he had previously owned, but what he now owned was all in one piece, and it was his alone. The village as a community now owned nothing, apart from some six acres of "charity land". There were no more "common rights". There were no more common interests. The village as a community no longer existed. There is scope here for the social historian, too. Has community life in the villages ever recovered from the effect of Enclosure? Would it have died in any case, had there been no Enclosure? Was there ever any real community life, other than that artificially imposed by the manorial system? I could pose many more questions — and answer none of them.

To John Bendysh, Esq. were allocated 800 acres; to William Hurrell 377. The discrepancy between this and my figure, given above, of nearly 500 acres is accounted for by allocations to his wife and son, by the Foxton House grounds, and by a startling difference discovered between estimated and actual acreage when the land was properly surveyed for the first time in history. Mary Rayner (sister of the Robert Rayner who had lived here) was allotted 1 acres 1 rood in Hopper Field (along the Barrington Road) "in lieu of right of common to a freehold cottage". What, in heaven's name, was an elderly spinster supposed to do with 1¼ acres? Grow turnips on it and keep a sheep or a cow, I suppose. Has any economic or agronomic theorist, I wonder, ever tried living on "one acre and a cow"? Of course, if old Mary Rayner had had a bit of foresight, and lived to be a hundred and ninety, she could have made a fortune from that bit of land — four building-plots at £1000 each! But she did not have the foresight, and she died in 1847, having sold the land for a few pounds.

Included in the allocation to William Elbourne was:

" — as and for Copyhold of the Manor of Foxtonbury with Wimbish and Chatteris — in lieu of and as compensation for all that cottage homestead and garden containing one rood and twenty-one perches allotted and awarded to William Hurrell, Esq.

"All that garden Orchard and homestead called Docwra's heretofore the property of John Bendyshe, Esq. containing three roods and eight perches, bounded on parts of the North-east and North-west by the next described Allotment, on the remaining part of the North-east by Foxton Green, on the South-east by the Public Drain called the Town Drain, on the South-east by the Public Drain called the Town Drain, on the South-west by the Farm homestead and home close belonging to the said William Elborne and on the remaining part of the North-west by the Town Street.

"And one other plot of land in Foxton Green of the breadth of Six feet containing one perch bounded on the N.E. by the said Green, on the S.E. and S.W. by the Cottage and Garden last awarded to the said William Elborne and on the N.W. by the Town Street."

So, this cottage was exchanged for the cottage occupied by the Pinks, opposite the Black Boy. The annexation of a strip of the Green is intriguing, and the ease with which it was done even more so. Was it prompted, I wonder, by the desire to keep the fair-ground activities — for the fair was still very much in evidence — from actually impinging upon the cottage? One can visualise the window-sills being used to support tankards and elbows, and the front door rendered unusable by a stall set right up against it. Or was it — and this seems more likely — that fencing of property had now become even more essential than ever, and space had to be provided for the planting of a hedge, with room left on the inside for the maintenance of the same? The hedge then planted was still there until about twenty years ago.

As for the occupants of the homestead called Docwra's, not a word. There might have been none, for all the Commissioners knew or cared. Actually there was an occupant, as we shall see presently. All that remains to be said on the subject of Enclosure is that it, along with its attendant circumstances, settled the status of this house for the next hundred years. The 1830 map shows one shed alone remaining of what had once been a full range of barn, stables etc. The one-time yeoman's estate was reduced to just over three-quarters of an acre. From now on it was a labourer's cottage. In the Land Tax Assessment return of 1839 it does not even officially exist.

CHAPTER XI
Isons and Heffers

I do not know who lived here after the death of Robert Rayner. In all probability the cottage stood empty for about five years, for the first, but not the last, time in its history.

In October 1829 Samuel Ison married Sarah Irons of Cambridge. He was then thirty-five years old, she twenty-nine. They had perhaps deferred marriage until such time as they could get a house, and I am assuming that the date of their marriage was the date of their coming here. At a rent of under two shillings a week, they had found a real bargain. That was the normal rent for a labourer's house, but this was something rather special in the way of labourer's houses. Samuel, like any other labourer, was unable to read or write. His wife could at least write her name. He was a shepherd, and remained a shepherd all his life. Whose flock he tended, I am not sure; probably that of William Heffer; possibly more than one man's flock. He soon began to acquire a flock of his own, all born in this cottage:

January	1834	Anne.
July	1835	Charles.
November	1837	Edward.
November	1838	Elizabeth.
November	1841	Mary Ann.
November	1845	William.
September	1848	Sarah.

Once again the old house was enlivened by childish squalling and squabbling, childish shouts and laughter. With a shepherd's wages at around £30 a year, Samuel Ison was well-off compared with most labourers, and could earn a bit extra at hay-time and harvest. His work was not hard much of the time, but of course he worked "all the hours that God sent", and when not busy with his sheep there was that large garden to be tended. A real boon, that, for it meant that he could grow all his own vegetables, especially potatoes, which were only now coming to be recognised as a useful addition to a working-class diet. (Soon to become the main item in that same diet!)

The full house, in mid-century, soon began to empty again. Sarah, the youngest, was the first to go, and the first Ison to be buried in Foxton; she only lived nine months. Anne, at the age of nineteen, married John Wright in 1853. Elizabeth died in 1856, aged eighteen. Mary Ann, also at the age of nineteen, married James Freeman in 1860. There was nothing sacred about the age of nineteen. A working-class girl got married as soon as she could (or as soon as she had to) in order to escape the drudgery and tension of a crowded household. Of course she promptly started a crowded household of her own, beset with even more drudgery. But that, being in the future, was not seen. What would happen to society, I wonder, if youth should ever come to look at life through the eyes of the aged?

Charles and Edward, the two eldest lads, moved out of the village, married no doubt, and settled elsewhere; there are Isons all over the county and in Cambridge.

Work was not always easy to get in a rural area in the mid-nineteenth century. There was more work, and more money, to be had in the towns. In particular there was good money to be earned, by men not afraid of hard work, on the construction of the railways. Foxton station was put into service in 1851 as a station on the Great Eastern line from Cambridge to Shepreth, where the Great Northern line from Royston terminated. The G.N.R. organised a coach service from Shepreth to Cambridge in competition with the trains of their rivals. One of the minor diversions of young William Ison must have been to watch the G.N.R. coach and horses held up by the G.E.R. train at Foxton crossing. William stayed on in the cottage with the old folks and worked for William Heffer, who lived at the farm next door.

And here we catch up with the Heffers. The "William Elborn" to whom the Enclosure allotment had been made was William Elborne the Youngest. His grandfather, William the Elder, had died in 1826; his father, William the Younger, died in 1824. There was a bit of a wrangle over the grandfather's will, in which the grandmother and the wife of William the Younger clashed. It was all sorted out by Time, as usual. Grandmother died in 1830; William the Youngest died in 1832, aged twelve, and the property passed jointly to two other grandsons, Henry Goode Elborne and Edward Pickhaven Elborne, both "infants", aged sixteen and twelve respectively, under the guardianship of their other grandfather. They had little interest in the property, which was let to William Heffer, who farmed it when Robert Rayner gave up. William Heffer also farmed Barrons, at the other end of the village, as did his son William Heffer the Younger. The latter in 1863, bought from the Elbornes:

> "All that Farmhouse, Barns, Stables, Cowhouse, and other Outbuildings, Labourer's Cottage, Orchard, Garden, etc. part freehold and part Heriotable Copyhold — "

The area of the cottage, garden and "orchard" was still 3 roods & 9 perches. The orchard had in fact been cleared, and in its place was a small paddock. The property was sold in two lots; the farmhouse and buildings went for £400; this cottage and all the land for £800. Three days later William Heffer mortgaged all the copyhold which included this cottage, for £600 — to Henry Goode Elborne! That gives some idea of the financial straits of farmers in the 1860s.

Back to the Isons, unaffected by this change of ownership, most likely unaware of it: William Ison married in 1865 at the age of twenty. There would appear to have been a certain degree of compulsion about the marriage, a common enough feature, then as now, but it turned out all right. Such marriages usually did, out of sheer necessity: I mean the sheer necessity of accepting things as they were. This acceptance need not be taken as indicative of low mentality or lack of spirit (both of which were common amongst the working-class, but by no means confined to them); rather of plain common-sense. Things were what they were, so you might as well make the best of them.

William was destined to surpass his father as a begetter of offspring. Here is his score, all born in this cottage:

October	1865	Charles.

September	1866	Elizabeth.
January	1869	Sarah Ann.
December	1869	Susannah.
March	1873	Maria.
December	1874	George Edward.
March	1878	Minnie and Thomas.
October	1879	Herbert.

A quiverful indeed! Where on earth did they all sleep? And what about the old folks? Actually the old folks had moved out when the house began to get too full, and had gone to live in one half of the cottage which stood opposite the end of Mortimers Lane. There old Sarah eked out a living by selling home-made boiled sweets until she died in 1868, and old Samuel lingered on until 1880.

But how did one feed such a family as William's on a labourer's wage — 12/- a week? The answer is obviously "not very well". They ate what they could get, when there was anything to get, and, when there wasn't, they went hungry. In actual fact, I have the verbal testimony of one of them that they rarely went hungry. Their main sustenance, apart from groceries which had to be bought, was what William Ison was able to produce by cultivating his unusually large garden and the allotment near the Station, for which he paid a rent of four shillings a year. Most of this land was planted with potatoes, no longer considered as primarily animal-food, but now the basic food of "peasants", here as in Ireland. Those potatoes, boiled and mashed, would also sustain a few pigs and fowls to supplement and enrich the family diet. "A good hunk o' fat bacon" was a breakfast much to be desired. It is unlikely that "butcher's meat" was often bought. Equally unlikely that William spent much time at the "Black Boy", though he must have retreated there occasionally to get away from that houseful of squalling kids, and he did in later life acquire a taste for rum and milk. His main worry, and that of his family, must have been to avoid illness, and that he seems to have done. Not so young Charles, though; he lost one of his legs in boyhood, an infirmity which severely limited his scope as a labourer; he often accompanied a shepherd on his rounds, and on occasion earned as much as ninepence a week as a bird-scarer! In the winter he would catch larks, which he sold.

William always managed to find work, which suggests that he was a good, steady worker. Like many others at this time, he was lured away from the "land" for a time by the high wages paid to the "coprolite" diggers at Barrington and in the river-meadows of Foxton. These "coprolites" were in fact nodules of almost pure phosphate of lime, found in a seam varying in thickness from a few inches to a couple of feet, at a depth varying from four feet to as much as twenty feet. When treated with sulphuric acid they produced a superphosphate highly valued as artificial fertiliser; they were worth £3 a ton, and an acre could yield as much as 300 tons. The land was leased for three years at £150 an acre, to be levelled and re-soiled at the end of the operation. All the digging was done by hand and spade, and paid for at piecework rates, so much per cubic yard removed. A good man — meaning a man as strong as an ox, with hands as tough as hippopotamus hide — could earn up to 40/- a week. This was a fantastic wage. The average, about 25/-

a week, was pretty good, good enough to justify a man spending a third of it on beer, which he could do without leaving the site, for an enterprising beer-seller had set up business on the spot.

Then there was, especially for the top-soil men, of whom old George Stock was one, the ever-present possibility of turning up something of archaeological or "antiquarian" value – an urn, a Roman amphora, a Saxon grave (hundreds were destroyed at Barrington and Haslingfield), ornaments and pottery – for which men like the Rev. E. Conybeare were willing to pay good money. One Roman jar earned the finders £5. This bonus money, needless to say, was invariably spent on beer! The local farmers, including William Heffer, were anything but pleased with this state of things. They were faced with the alternative of raising the agricultural wage, recently fallen to as little as 10/- a week, to double that amount, or losing all their men except the work-shy. And this just at a time when depression was once more setting in, due to imports of corn from overseas. Of course the coprolite boom was short-lived; the seam was exhausted, and anyway it was soon possible to import from America phosphates at far lower cost. But it was good while it lasted.

The accommodation in the cottage was not strained to the extent which might appear likely, though it had become necessary to convert one of the bedrooms into two by building a partition down the centre, and the close-packed state of beds in the other bedroom is still attested by worn places in the floor-boards. The twins, Minnie and Thomas, lived only just long enough to be baptised in the house; the girl died five days, the boy fourteen days after birth. Susannah left home to go to work at Walton, in domestic service; she died at the age of twenty-two and was buried at Foxton, the officiating minister being the Rev. E. Conybeare of Barrington. Sarah Ann also went away "in service", and married outside the village. Elizabeth never married, but came within reach of matrimony, for the records show that she had a daughter, Grace Minnie, in September 1894. She survived this social stigma with admirable aplomb – and it took quite a bit of nerve to do that in a village in late Victorian days – for, after a period of domestic service in Cambridge, she came back to the cottage, and when she died in 1917 at the age of fifty-three she was granted the rare distinction of having her address entered in the parish register: "The Green, Foxton." For the greater part of Herbert's youth, then, there were three children and their parents living in the cottage. Before I tell the story of Herbert, I will catch up on the Heffers.

I have not recounted the saga of the six cottages in Stockers Lane (now Station Road); one house originally, later converted into a double cottage, then four more added. Nor shall I. I only mention them here to explain the extraordinary situation which confronted me in 1946 when, in order to buy one house, I had to buy six. They were sold in 1872 to Robert Allen Heffer, son of William the Younger, who needed them to house labourers, or to attract labourers and then house them. In 1875 William Heffer paid off the mortgage of 12 years previous. There never seems to have been any great hurry, on the part of the borrower, still less on the part of the lender, to clear these mortgages, which were as common then as Building Society loans are now. The reason was, no doubt, that the land was safer than a bank for the lender; and as for the borrower, he doubtless hoped for a rise in the price of corn, or a bumper harvest, or a miracle. William Heffer was out of debt, Robert Allen slipping into it. Few farmers at this period could keep clear of debt.

William Heffer lived much of his life at the farm next door, but when he died in 1892 it was being farmed by William Moore. His will, dated 1887, is a good example of how to ensure a family row. All the Foxton property, including this cottage, was left to Robert Allen Heffer, then to William Robert (Robert Allen's eldest son) at the age of twenty-one. If William Robert died before the age of twenty-one, it was to go to the first son of Robert Allen to reach the age of twenty-one. If Robert Allen had no sons who reached the age of twenty-one, then it was to go to all the daughters of Robert Allen who reached the age of twenty-one, or who married under the age of twenty-one. As flagrant a case as one could wish of unintentional incitement to homicide or abduction, or both. In the event, neither occurred. This cottage, incidentally, is still called "Docwra's" in the record of enrolment of Robert Allen's succession in 1895, and still 3 roods 9 perches in area.

Robert Allen Heffer farmed and lived at Barrons, where he had the house re-constructed, then moved to the farm next door and had that largely rebuilt. He was unlucky in his timing. The flow of cheaply imported grain and farm-produce from the U.S.A. and the British Empire became a flood. Because of advances in machine technique, large-scale capitalisation, relatively low production costs, and improved transportation, it was cheaper to supply Britain with grain, beef, mutton, hides and wool from thousands of miles away than from the fields and farms at home. This went on until the First World War temporarily halted the flood. British agriculture had known depression before — several times in the 19th century — but this was nearly fatal. If farming had not been for many a "way of life" to which they were born and from which they could not escape, it is certain that large tracts of land would have gone out of cultivation. Instead, the farmers struggled on, on borrowed money, hoping for better times. The land was always there, and land was money. Unfortunately, it was not the kind of money with which you paid your men (and, God knows, they were paid little enough!) or bought your stock, seeds and implements. Robert Allen was hardest hit just when he had the right to expect a life of some leisure and security. He borrowed steadily from 1894 to 1914. To no avail. He retired to Surrey, a very sick man, and made his will on July 5th 1915; a model of brevity:

"I desire that all my possessions be equally divided among my wife and son." He died the next day.

Before we consider the effect of those two irreconcilable wills, let us follow the Ison fortunes to their conclusion.

CHAPTER XII
Tim Ison

Tim Ison — he was christened Herbert, but nobody, to my knowledge, ever called him anything but Tim — was born here in October 1879. His grandfather died five months later at the age of eighty-six. The old man could have told the uncomprehending infant tales of the Battle of Waterloo and "Boneypart". The child, had he been able to speak, and been gifted with the necessary vision, could have stunned the old man with tales of atomic bombs and machines which flew faster than sound. More than that, he could have really alarmed him by telling about a machine which would reap and thresh corn in one operation! Their joint lives were to span 176 years.

In 1883, after long delay, a Board School was opened in Foxton with "accommodation for 100 scholars", i.e. there was room for a hundred if they all stood still. The average attendance was around the 70 mark, and amongst them was young Tim Ison. Occasionally. A boy of six or seven could find so many things to do which were so much more interesting than school: such as bird-nesting, stone-picking, bird-scaring, watching the horses, minding the sheep, raiding orchards, picking potatoes, catching larks, gleaning, etc., etc. At some of those occupations you could earn a penny, sometimes, if you were lucky. Whereas you actually had to *pay* to go to school — one whole penny per week! No wonder the attendance was "irregular". No wonder "the majority of the children in Standard One knew little or nothing". This is no reflection on Miss Corlett, the courageous and devoted headmistress. She taught a large number of children to read, write and reckon. Tim Ison was not one of them; he never did learn to read or write, then or later.

When it came to doing a useful job of work, though, Tim was just the boy. When, for instance, old Mr. Stanford (father of Bill Stanford, who last thatched the cottage) was renewing the whole thatch, a process necessitating a new "bed" of reeds and the securing of the first layer of straw to the rafters by means of strong twine, it was young Tim who stood on the inside and thrust the long needle back through the thatch, then pulled the strings tight. (Many of those strings are still there). Or when the brick oven needed to be cleaned out, Tim was of the right size and disposition to clamber through the iron door — a thing he often did "for a lark". "It was nice and warm in there". He slept in one of the bedrooms overlooking Home Farm. The floor of the bedroom, he told me, often needed repairing; which is not surprising — it had been there for 300 years!

Tim could not recall ever being hungry. Of course he was hungry every day, at every meal-time, but he did not remember being unable to satisfy his hunger. When, long afterwards, he was asked what he used to eat in the early days, he just could not remember. There was "always something". They used to "make do with what there was". That phrase, which Tim must have heard often, and later used regularly, sums up the whole of the Ison philosophy. All his life he was to make do with what there was, accept what life happened to send, without questioning, without grumbling ("mustn't grumble" was one of his stock phrases),

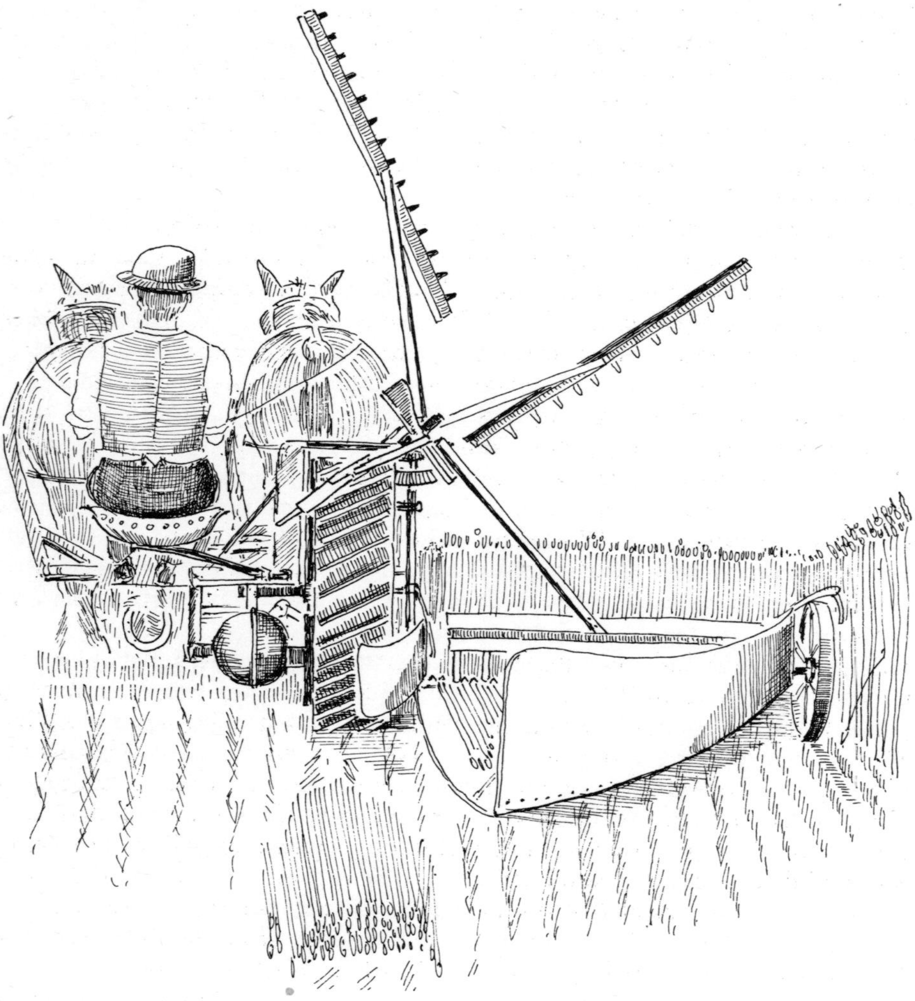

Fig. 14 The "old chucker-out".

without undue gratitude for the unexpected favour when it came.

William Ison at this time was horse-keeper for William Asplin at Herods Farm, a responsible job which he did well; he "kept a good stable", and set the boys a good example, which Tim was keen to follow. He began work, officially, in 1891, at the age of twelve, being employed as a farm-boy by Robert Allen Heffer at Barrons. His wage was 3/- (three shillings!) per week. There were always six days in the week, and often seven; seventy hours work in a week was not uncommon. You will have calculated that Tim was paid at the rate of just over one halfpenny an hour! And this was at a time when farmers found it virtually impossible to make farming pay. Bear in mind, too, that a boy of twelve on a farm did not stand around idle half the time, or "make the tea". I have heard many a farmer remark that "A boy is as good as a man." (They usually went on to say that two boys were only half as good as one, and that three boys were no damn good at all!)

Tim did not stay with Mr. Heffer. There was no bond of loyalty between master and man, or master and boy. For a time he worked with his father at Asplin's. He remembered spending whole days in the barn, threshing corn with a flail. In those days before the self-binder was in general use (the first in Foxton was introduced by Mr. Gifford of the Bury in about 1895) barley was harvested loose and stored in the barn. As the pile accumulated it was trodden firm by a horse walking round and round on it. At the end of the day the horse was lowered down from his lofty perch near the roof by a system of ropes, pulleys and slings! The immediate predecessor of the binder was the "sail reaper" (as I knew it in my boyhood; Tim called it the "old chucker-out"), a horse-drawn machine which cut the corn and threw it aside in hundles, which were gathered and tied, if the crop were wheat, oats, beans or rye. Tim and his father talked of smashing this machine, for it was going to put a lot of scythingmen out of a job. It was only talk, though. They did not dare put their threat into effect. Jobs were too precious to be thrown away in that mad fashion.

And often jobs were difficult to find. One harvest-time Tim and three others from Foxton walked daily to Chrishall Grange, a distance of over five miles, setting out at six o'clock each morning. On the way home at the end of a long day, they would manage to reach the "Queen's Head" at Fowlmere five minutes before closing-time. You can bet that they put those five minutes to good use! Another year, having finished harvest here, they went into the Fens and did another stint; harvest was usually later there owing to the late drying-out of the land in the spring.

Tim was willing to tackle any job, however dirty or unpleasant it might be. As he himself said, "If you didn't do it, somebody else would". And if somebody else did it, you had lost a job. He worked for a time at the Barrington brickworks – a by-product of the coprolite digging. He joined his brother George in London, and helped in the construction of the Rotherhithe Tunnel. He worked at the "Angle" (East Anglian) cement-works at Shepreth, then at the "Dreadnought" (later to become Eastwoods) in Barrington, helping to build the bridge which carried the light railway over the river. He worked anywhere where there was work to be done: especially heavy work. He was never ill, and as strong as an ox.

On one occasion, when a dray laden with ten hundredweight of coal on the front was found to be obstructing the passage of other carts, he took hold of the back end and moved it bodily to one side.

Tim never did any courting — "nor anything like that". He never talked to or about women. The other sex, apart from his mother and sisters, did not exist.

Then came the First World War. Tim was in the Suffolk Regiment from 1916 to the end of the war, and saw service in the trenches. He mentioned Ypres and Nancy; he told of putting the feet of his bed in tins of diesel-oil to stop the invasion of bugs; he told how one of his mates would keep lifting his head to take a swig from a can, despite Tim's warning, and got a bullet through the can and his head. Apart from that, those ghastly years seem to have left little trace on his memory. He hardly ever talked of his war experiences, but there can be little doubt that he would make an ideal soldier; he would obey orders, do whatever had to be done, and keep out of trouble.

On demobilisation in 1919 he returned to Foxton, to rejoin Charles, George and his parents in the cottage. Things were much the same, except that the garden had been reduced to less than half its former size. The Heffers had had thoughts of selling the cottage before the war; a valuation of 1914 described it thus:

> "A Copyhold cottage containing two downstairs rooms and Kitchen, and three bedrooms, with large garden having a large frontage to the High Street, and containing one rood, let to Mr. Ison at £4. 10. 0. per annum, Landlord paying rates."

William Robert Heffer and Mrs. Julia Heffer, his mother, could not agree as to the ownership of the property. Mrs. Heffer naturally claimed the validity of her late husband's will. William Robert backed his grandfather's will. Neither really wanted the property, but both wanted the money which it represented. The only way out of the dilemma was to sell the lot. The farmhouse and land was sold in 1915 to Mr. Dobbin. On July 4th 1919, the six cottages in Station Road and this cottage were sold by public auction at the "Black Boy". The terminology of the Bill of Sale is amusing: — "valuable properties" — "capital cottages" — "good gardens" — "convenient cottage" — "large kitchen". Those phrases, of course, were written by the seller, not the buyer! Two other details caught my eye: "Mr. Ison, whose tenancy expires at Michaelmas next", and "Tenant claims fowlhouses in garden, stove in kitchen and oven door". The whole seven cottages were bought by Edward Hirschhorn of Wood Green, London, blindmaker, for £520. Of that amount, this cottage and garden contributed £70. Old Mrs. Dobbin once told me that she could have bought the cottage for seventy pounds. I did not believe her then. I find it difficult to believe even now, when confronted by the hard facts. Seventy pounds! Why, I could get that much today for the oven-door, which, by the way, was not claimed by the tenant, but is still here.

Neither was old William Ison given notice to quit. Edward Hirschhorn did nothing whatever with the cottages — (he collected the rent, I suppose) — except leave them to his son Charles, also a blindmaker. Tim's mother died in 1921 at the age of seventy-nine. Maria came home to look after her father and brothers. Tim and Charles, despite his wooden leg, looked after the garden and kept it in wonderful shape. This was the one passion in Tim's life — if passion is not too inappropriate a word. No one could grow earlier lettuces or bigger cabbages than he. He planted greengage trees, all of which were still there until recently. Despite their common interest in gardening, Tim and Charles did not always get on well together. They both had a fiery temper. In Tim it smouldered all day and hardly showed if he was left alone, apart from a sullen silence. In Charles it would burst into flame, fed rather than quenched by beer, and woe betide any who crossed him, wooden leg or no wooden leg! On one occasion an adversary, requested to "come outside", found himself confronting an irate Charles leaning against the pub wall and brandishing that same wooden leg! Tim did not drink a lot. He liked his few pints on Saturday nights in the summer, and in later life one pint at mid-day on a Sunday. He never got drunk, and was only once known to go "wild", one Saturday night when he got on the swings at Foxton Fair (no longer held on the Green) and tried to send the swing-boat over the top.

In 1928 old William, tired of life, and, at eighty-three, with nothing more to live for, tried to cut his throat. His skin was too tough ("like walrus hide", said Dr. Young) and his hand too weak. He lived on for another two years. It was not until 1932 that Charles Hirschhorn gave Tim and Maria notice to quit, which they did. Tim sometimes spoke of this event with as much anger as I ever heard him express, evidently having forgotten, or never having understood, that it was his father, not he, who had been guaranteed tenancy of the cottage. So ended Tim's fifty-three years in the cottage. He and his brothers and sister went to live in the cottage opposite the vicarage, where he continued to tend his garden, and went on working for Stocks, where he had worked since the war. George died in 1940, Charles in 1947, Maria in 1956. Soon after Maria's death Tim "stopped work", at the age of seventy-six, and lived alone.

I was privileged to know him well, and spent many days working with him in the fields at harvest-time. Many was the time we shared a shock ("stook" or "stouk" in other regions; non-existent now) as we ate our elevenses or tea. Tim would never collapse clumsily onto a shock, as most men did; he always took one of the end sheaves and laid it flat as a seat, with the upright sheaves at his back, and always replaced the sheaf when he got up to resume work. That was merely one detail which marked Tim as different. It was not just that he was an old man, whereas most of the others were young. His attitude to work was different. His attitude towards the horses, the tools, the corn which he handled was not the same as that of the others. He handled corn as though it were *his* corn, though he knew only too well that it wasn't. When setting-up shocks, he would never leave a sheaf which the binder had failed to tie, but carefully gather it with his hands and tie it with a "band" of twisted straw – exactly as his medieval ancestors had done. His hand-tied sheaves were easily recognisable, and always provoked the same ribald comment from someone on the corn-stack – "one of old Tim's" – but Tim's straw-bands never came untied.

He never hurried. He never, to my knowledge, made an unnecessary movement. He was never late. His pace at the end of the day was what it had been at the start of the day. That pace, it need hardly be said, was not very fast; it was his own pace. Yet Tim somehow seemed to get as much work done as many of the younger fellows. The latter frequently chaffed him, and Tim shrugged off most of their banter in silence. I have since learned, from one who knew him better than I did, that he was more offended than he appeared to be. I never heard him swear, because I never saw him really angry. Nor did I ever see him twist the red handkerchief, which he invariably wore round his neck, a gesture which, coupled with the deep purple hue assumed by his bulging neck, was a warning to would-be baiters and aggressors that things had gone quite far enough. His loyalty was firstly to his fellow-workers, even when he did not like them. He would cover up their mistakes or slackness, and if, despite this, they were found out, he would meet inquiries with an impassive "I don't know". But, in a real emergency, there was no more loyal or more dependable servant. When a broken elbow robbed the horses of their usual attendant, Tim, without being asked, was there, with a grunted "Leave the horses to me".

For some reason which no one has managed to explain, he did not like children, never had liked children. He would never work with a boy if he could avoid doing so. When there were young lads in the team, Tim would always sit apart from the others at break-time. That was how he and I came to spend so much time together. Then, as he munched away at his bread and cheese, open clasp-knife in one hand, or sipped his cold tea, he liked to chat about the old days. He had to be prompted before the slow reminiscences would emerge, punctuated at intervals by "in them days". His words came more easily, though less audibly, when his stubby little old pipe was charged with "bacca" and drawing well; or when the surreptitiously inserted quid of tobacco in his cheek was generating a nicotine-impregnated brew which, but for his equally surreptitious expectorations, would have killed him years ago. He was only ill once, after he had stopped working, and had to be taken to hospital almost by force.

He was what the world — the sophisticated, superficial world of today — would call not very bright. But he was not stupid or ignorant. Far from it. Narrow-minded, if you like; if by that you mean that his knowledge and views were circumscribed by the bounds of his own personal experience. Within those bounds was a depth of understanding beyond his powers of expression. Anything outside that experience was dismissed with the formula, "I'm sure I don't know". He knew, for instance, nothing of barometers, but he could tell you when a change of weather was coming, especially frost or thaw, by observing the movements of birds. He resented change, when it affected him. When change did not affect him, he ignored it.

Tim died on November 28th 1968, in Linton Hospital, at the age of ninety. He was not of these times. He was one of the last survivors of medieval England, of a race of peasants born to work, living to work, happy in work; seeing no sense, no real meaning, in anything but work.

"Poor fool!" did I hear someone say?

Tim was not poor. Nor was he a fool.

Fig. 15 Tim.

CHAPTER XIII
War and Post-war

And so the cottage reflected yet another change in the social order. It became a "week-end cottage", a place where jaded townsmen could get away from it all, a rural refuge to which they could retreat from the attack upon their nerves made by traffic, noise, smells, people, hustle and bustle – town life, in fact. Time matters less in the country, people are fewer, smells are different – well, they *were* different, twenty-five years ago.

Large-scale alteration and improvements were needed in the cottage before it could measure up to the standards of Londoners going rustic, if only at week-ends. There was, in 1932, no electricity in the cottage, no plumbing, no water, no heating, no "sanitation". (The little black shed half-way down the garden had served generations of Rayners and Isons, and doubtless served them well, but Londoners' love of rusticity did not extend *that* far!) Apart from the brick oven which one of the Rayners had put in, and the renewal of the thatch, the cottage was exactly as Samuel Campion had left it two hundred and fifty years previously.

The modernisation was done by local builders, as cheaply as possible, working on the principle that "what the eye doesn't see, the heart doesn't grieve". One half of the space behind the chimney-stack was converted into a bathroom and W.C., the other half into a kitchen of sorts; a wooden ceiling was inserted, and water-storage tanks installed in the space above, supplying bathroom, kitchen and central-heating system. The water still had to be brought from the pump on the Green in a two-wheeled watercart, such as nearly everyone in the village used in those days, and pumped up to the tanks by a hand-operated rotary pump. The old brick oven was demolished – the door being preserved as a memento – and a new fireplace and chimney built inside the original chimney, which was left intact. A wrought-iron fire-basket, supported by authentic-looking andirons, was specially made for a grate. This part of the work was very well done indeed. Beside the new chimney, but still inside the old one, was an "Ideal" boiler for heating water and supplying the four radiators; it proved to be far from ideal, and had to be scrapped later. Electric light was installed. A new floor was put in the south bedroom. The under-side of the thatch, between the rafters, was plastered – this must have been very difficult to do, and the finish was rather rough, as was only to be expected – and the topmost few feet were boarded in to make bedroom ceilings. A cess-pit, of sorts, was made on the far side of the garden; it was, fortunately, never subjected to official inspection. A garage was built at the bottom of the garden. The garden itself was re-planned to include a lawn and flower-beds – (that would have amused Thomas Campion!). The thatch was patched up and given a protecting cover of wire-netting – (*that* would have delighted all the Campions and Rayners!). The walls were coated with pebble-dash at the gable-ends where the thatch gave least protection, and the whole exterior colour-washed a sort of burnt sienna. On the whole a worthy effort, despite the flaws. It did at least save the cottage from extinction. Another few years, two decades at most, and demolition – or a rebuilding amounting to almost the same thing – would have been the only practical course to take.

What went on at those week-ends in the cottage in the 1930s is none of my business. I have heard tales of "rare goings-on", which I will not repeat. You know how country people love to gossip. All I will say is that, from an obscure nettle-infested corner at the back of the potting-shed, I cleared away over four hundred empty bottles. There was no refuse-collection in those days, so they presented a bit of a problem. I ought, in fairness, to add that the Hirschhorns showed an active interest in village affairs; "Charlie" is still remembered and spoken of with affection by many in the village.

On Mary 24th 1938, occurred an historic event in the life of the cottage. An Agreement made between John Nelson Bendyshe, Esq. of Exbourne, Devon, and Charles Hirschhorn of Wood Green, London, declared that:

> "Whereas the manorial incidents in respect of the said land were extinguished on the first day of January 1936, by virtue of Section 138 (i)(c) of the Law of Property Act, 1922 – (better late than never!) – now it is hereby witnessed that the said John Nelson Bendyshe and the Land Owner hereby agree as follows: The compensation payable in respect of the extinguishment of the manorial incidents formerly affecting the said land shall be the sum of £76. 15. 8. and in respect of the mineral and other rights shall be the sum of 7/6 – The said John Nelson Bendyshe – hereby grants and conveys unto the Land Owner all the mines and minerals, if any, in or under the said land – ".

So the property became freehold. Note that it is the *land* which is being freed from the hand of manorial custom; there is no mention of a house. As for the mines and minerals, all I have ever found is gravel. Still, it is nice to know that, if there were an oil-well, or a coal-seam in the garden, it would be all mine!

The pleasures, indeed the possibility, of week-ending declined with the advent of the war. Black-out, petrol-rationing, extra duties, uncertainty – all served to keep people at home. In January 1940, Hirschorn sold this cottage, and the six others, to one E. H. Fisher for £400. He must have been desperately anxious to get rid of them, for he stood to lose heavily on the deal. Perhaps it was a sudden attack of "war nerves". We were all a bit like that in those days. The war was still in its "phoney" stage, but real war might come at any moment; London might be destroyed, even Foxton might be destroyed, property could be requisitioned, people uprooted and sent anywhere. There was an atmosphere of unreality about everything. Things looked much the same as usual, but you knew that they were not the same. Worst of all was the uncertainty. So that, when the real war did come, it was almost a relief. We knew then what we were in for – "blood, toil, tears and sweat". In early 1940 we did not know, and we were all jittery; especially Mr. Fisher. No sooner had he bought the seven cottages than he asked Hirschhorn to buy them back. He was liable to be conscripted any day, and property, to him, seemed "more of a liability than an asset", especially a cottage standing empty. "The cottage in Foxton Street", he wrote, "is of little value." It is some comfort to me to know that there is in the world at least one other man with as little business-sense as I have. I rather think that Charlie, his business instinct coming to the fore, knew what he was doing when he so readily bought back the property for the same price as he had sold it for.

It was indeed a good move, as soon became apparent. During the autumn and winter which followed, London was not a very healthy place to be in, and this cottage provided a perfect refuge from the bombing-raids. Here one could sleep in peace and security. It is true that a stick of bombs straddled the village one night in November 1940, but that was probably a mistake, and no damage was done. Later, the cottage was occupied by an R.A.F. officer from Bassingbourne. So it was not empty for very long.

Then we arrived on the scene.

I was demobilised in March 1946 and returned to England after 3½ years continuous service abroad with but one thought in my mind – to acquire a home and live in it, live there for the rest of my days. I had never had a home of my own. During the last six years I had "lived" in tents and huts, in camps, barracks, bivouacs – always on the move. I had lived in half a dozen different countries – Algeria, Tunisia, Italy, Yugoslavia, Egypt, Palestine, Syria, to say nothing of my travels about this country. All very marvellous, and I was utterly sick of it. I never wanted to travel again – well, not just yet, anyway. My job was waiting for me; I wanted a home within reach of it.

My assets at this stage were: a tidy sum of money which had accumulated during the war years, ninety days' leave, an old car which still ran well, petrol-coupons for about 500 miles, a good supply of portable provisions including a stuffed pork-chine supplied by my mother, a one-inch O.S. Map of the Cambridge area, and almost unlimited confidence. Based on a Cambridge hotel, we set out, my wife and I, on our home-finding expedition. We called on every estate-agent in the town, looked at numerous houses in Cambridge now selling at ten times what they had cost to build just before the war, and soon decided that we had better make for the open country. We set ourselves a limit of a fifteen-mile radius from Cambridge, and proceeded to explore this huge circle – actually a half-circle, for we ruled out the north – sector by sector. At village after village we enquired at post-offices, pubs, shops; we asked anybody and everybody; "Any houses for sale?", "Any houses empty?", "Has anyone just died?", "Anyone look like dying soon – say tomorrow or the day after?" Everywhere we met friendliness, sympathy and co-operation. But no home. By the afternoon of the third day we had visited 47 villages; the stuffed chine had all gone; the petrol-coupons down to the last half-dozen; and our confidence at a very low ebb indeed. It was then that we came to Foxton.

"Yes," said the good lady at the Post Office, "there is an empty cottage on the Green and I think it is for sale." Two minutes later we were on the Green, peering through the windows. We did not go inside. There was no need to. We were desperate, and, at that moment, too excited to think about all the common-sense things which one ought to do when buying a house. Miss Stock at Home Farm gave us the name and address of the owner. The London Directory at the G.P.O., Cambridge, gave us his telephone number. Thank heaven he wasn't called Smith – we should have wasted a precious half-hour finding him! There were only two Hirschhorns in the whole of London! The phone was answered immediately. Everything was going my way. Yes, the cottage was for sale; he didn't want to sell it, but his wife did (bless her!); there were six other cottages which would have

Fig. 16 The pump on the Green. Erected by Canon Selwyn in 1872. In use until 1965.

to be bought with it (bit of a shock, that, but my confidence was at the peak). The price? Two thousand two hundred and fifty.

You who may be reading this, and who have recently bought a house, will no doubt gasp at that figure. I did – but for a totally different reason from yours. Quickly recovering my composure, I said "Right, I'll buy." I wrote a letter that evening to confirm my offer, and got an immediate reply. Then followed several days of acute anxiety. Had I done something very sensible, or was I completely crazy?

The next three weeks were weeks of hectic activity, interspersed with impatient and helpless inactivity, as we waited for solicitors to get a move on. Every penny we possessed, and quite a lot that we did not possess, was pressed into service. In-laws rallied nobly to the cause; the Bank was more than co-operative. We moved in on April 26th 1946. For three days, before the arrival of our furniture, we had bedding, a borrowed mattress, enough crockery and cutlery for a picnic meal, a table and two chairs loaned by the Stocks, and nothing else. On the second day the vicar called to bless the house. Silently, we blessed the vicar.

We soon got down to the task of making the house habitable and the garden presentable and productive. Which, come to think of it, is what we have been doing ever since. Old Tom Stock with his scythe tackled the grass on the lawn, now over two feet high. I was presented with a whole hundredweight of seed-potatoes, and bunged them all in, fighting a battle all the way against the weeds. The nettles could wait for another year – anyway there were broody hens, and soon chirping chicks, who had come to regard the nettles as their home. That first winter of 1946-47 was pretty bad, the severest I have ever known, perhaps the severest the cottage has ever known. There seemed no way of preventing the east wind from blowing right through the house; pipes froze, then burst; getting water was a nightmare. But we survived, and, looking back on it, I think we were as happy then as we have ever been. We were home.

The six other cottages presented a real problem. I did not want them – I don't think anybody wanted them, or ever had. I called once to collect the rents, then sat down to do a bit of simple arithmetic. It was clear that, what with interest on the mortgage, rates, Schedule A Tax, to say nothing of the cost of repairs which, as my tenants were quick to inform me, were urgently needed, ownership of those cottages was costing me more than £30 a year. That is assuming that I collected the rents. Having done it once, I knew I could never do it again, and I never did. I was determined to sell, at any price, preferably at one which would enable me to clear my mortgage. Within two months I sold them, all six, for £500. The purchaser sold them a year later for £600. A few years later *one* of them sold for £900. And I couldn't care less!

CHAPTER XIV
A new roof

In 1955 the thatch was in need of repair – not merely repair, but renewal. The wire-netting had rusted away in many places, and the sparrows were not slow to take advantage of the excellent nesting-sites thus made available to them. It was not actually leaking anywhere, but I was convinced that it soon would. There were at that time several experienced thatchers still alive and operating in the locality, all much in demand and with more work on their hands than they could manage. When I approached Bill Stanford of Shepreth, a man then already in his sixties, he did not seem in any great hurry to take on the job. He came to look at the cottage – not that that was really necessary, for he knew every thatched roof for miles around – and pronounced that it was good for a few years yet. I persisted in my request that he should do the work, and at last he agreed, influenced partly by the fact that it had been his father who had last thatched the cottage, but mainly by a novel bargain which he was able to strike with me. He had been asked, and had agreed, to thatch an old cottage at Shepreth, then being restored, and had had some difficulty about getting the straw. There was no lack of straw in those days, only Bill Stanford liked to choose the straw which he intended to use. He had seen a crop of wheat growing alongside the main road between Foxton station and Shepreth, had seen it threshed, and had examined the straw-stack. *That* was the straw which he wanted! George Smith was rather reluctant to let him have it, or part of it, because George wanted it for his own use – good straw made good muck! So, Stanford would thatch my cottage, if I could persuade George to let him have enough of that straw to thatch the Shepreth cottage, and enough for mine as well. Which, fortunately, I managed to do.

In April 1956 the Green disappeared beneath three wagon-loads of straw. Soon there was straw, it seemed, everywhere. The old thatch made far more mess than the new. It seemed to consist mainly of dust and broken "spits". For four weeks I had a bonfire at the bottom of the garden every day. Daily clearing-up was the only way to prevent the garden from disappearing as the Green had done. The volume of old stuff which came off the roof amazed me, and yet it was a mere fraction of what was left on. Only in a few places was it necessary to remove the old thatch down to the rafters; over most of the roof the old straw was perfectly sound about eight inches from the surface, though much of it had been there for fifty years or more. And it was perfectly dry. This is something which I still do not fully understand. I knew that, when stacking corn, the sheaves at the top of the stack had to be laid at a steep angle to throw off the rain, and that a properly-made stack never got wet. But a corn-stack only stood for a year at most; a thatch roof had to withstand twenty years and more of wind and rain. Moreover, I was convinced that the removal of the old thatch, and the hammering-in of the "spits" to secure the new thatch, would bring down most of the plaster which had been applied to the inside between the rafters. To my relief and amazement, not one scrap of plaster was displaced. This again I do not understand. It could only be that the straw was so well laid and so firmly packed that it is virtually solid.

I naturally wished to learn all I could about the art of thatching. Not that I had any intention of ever trying to practise it – I couldn't endure those hours of standing on a ladder, the carrying of heavy wet bundles on my back, the cruel punishment inflicted on the hands by sharp sticks, sharp straw, rough wire, cold winds. We often admire – and if we don't, it is high time we did – the skill and devotion of these old craftsmen; thatchers, wheelwrights, smiths, hedgers, members of a rapidly vanishing fraternity. What we tend to forget, it seems to me, is that foremost amongst their admirable qualities was toughness. They were men of iron and wood and leather in more senses than one. Before they could develop their skill and display their devotion they had to learn to overcome physical discomfort and weakness. Not to ignore it – that would have resulted in injury – but to minimise its effect by learning to do a hard job in the most efficient way, the "right" way. That is why their work always looked "easy" to an uninitiated observer.

No, I wanted to learn about thatching because this was the first, and last, opportunity I should ever have. I set about it in what I thought was the obvious way, by asking "Why?" – and thereby learnt nothing about thatching, but something about Bill Stanford. For several days I just could not get a clear or civil answer to my "Why are you doing that?" or "Why do you do it that way?" Then it dawned on me. To ask him why he was doing something was tantamount to suggesting that he ought *not* to do it, or that he ought to do it differently. I have since noticed the same reaction in others of his generation. So I changed my approach and put my questions in the form of suggestions or suppositions, making them as intelligent as I could. Whereupon he was able to confirm or confute my suggestions, to his entire satisfaction in either case, and we got along famously.

In common with all craftsmen, he was better at showing than at telling. He showed me how to "shake out" the straw to start with, to remove any grain or chaff which might be left in it. Then, from the heap of shaken straw, thoroughly soaked with buckets of water, to "pull out" by the handfull and lay the straws all in one direction. This was "gathered" with a rake and tied in a bundle of the right size to be carried up the ladder and placed in the right spot to be within easy reach for doing one piece of roof. He told me one thing which directly contradicted a statement which I have seen repeated in book after book dealing with country matters, namely that the best straw for thatching is long straw. Long straw may be best – may have been best – for thatching corn-stacks, but the best straw for roofs is *short,* said Bill Stanford. I took his word for it, and still do. Certainly the straw which he used on my roof was short, and he described it as "the best straw he had ever handled".

My part in the operation stopped short at the foot of the ladder. I watched him take a handful of straw, grasp it firmly at one end, secure that to the "bed" with a split hazel-stick bent and twisted to a hairpin shape, lay another bunch alongside it, then another, until he had covered with four or five bunches an area about a yard wide and about a foot deep. I never did manage to calculate how many of those hazel-sticks there were in the whole roof – it must be thousands. And those thousands of "spits" were all selected, cut, split and sharpened by Stanford himself, in the evenings when he got home. Every morning he would arrive on his

Fig. 17 Bill Stanford.

bicycle with a bundle sufficient to last him through the day. One could tell – one was not so tactless as to ask – whether he intended to work a long or a short day merely by looking at the bundle of spits. The length of his day was determined by the circumstances, by the nature of the particular part of the roof where he was working. The clock had little or nothing to do with it.

In fact, he didn't have a watch. He may have possessed one, but he did not carry it at work. He would ask the time perhaps three times a day, and when he did, it meant either that he was ready for a cup of tea or that he was going to walk down to the pub to get some tobacco or matches. He rolled his own cigarettes, which he smoked incessantly on the job. My wife and I were somewhat alarmed at this, until he pointed out that you couldn't set fire to wet straw! We discovered quite soon that his frequent visits to the pub had another object – to keep an eye on the workmanship and progress of a rival who was thatching another cottage in the village! His comments on the other man's work were amongst the few remarks he ever made without prompting.

It took him about five weeks – during which he was held up by only one wet day – to complete the laying. Then came the trimming, the cutting of a decorative wavy line (his "signature") below the ridge, and, finally, the wiring. It was a beautiful job. He had said, before we made the contract, "Well, I can thatch it, or I can *thatch* it". He meant, as I realised, that he could do the job as cheaply as possible, or he could do it as well as possible. There was only the intonation of his voice to distinguish between the two. I said I wanted it *thatched,* and added £10 to the figure he quoted. He *thatched* it! Not only to my satisfaction, but, far more important, to his satisfaction. A week after the completion of the work he called in one Sunday afternoon with his wife. He "wanted to show her" my tomato-plants, which had aroused his scorn in the first place because I had put them out (under cloches) before the end of April, then his wonder and admiration because, despite late frosts, they were in flower before the end of May. I have always suspected, as I did then, that he really wanted her to see his masterpeice of craftsmanship. I do not blame him. He had every right to be proud of it.

CHAPTER XV
Life in the Cottage

Living in a really old house which was built for living in a very different age and a different way must, inevitably, involve some snags and problems. The greatest snag of all is the sheer age of much of the fabric. At no time in its history has the cottage ever undergone a complete restoration. Materials which have been there for hundreds of years must obviously be constantly crumbling from age and decay; this applies particularly to the infilling of lath and plaster between the studs. The time will come when I shall have to stop patching here and there, have the whole wall stripped and replastered over expanded metal, or something better. But I do not consider it a very urgent matter, particularly as it is the outside which is affected most; inside, the walls are dry and relatively very sound. And there is a certain satisfaction in knowing that, if for any reason I were trapped in the house, I could escape by kicking a hole in the wall!

It is difficult to keep the house clean, having been built in an age when cleanliness was a long way behind godliness. All houses, I suppose, get dirty if they are properly used, i.e. used for living in and not for looking at. This one gets more dirty more quickly. When the north wind blows, it blows down the chimney – only the north wind; all other winds go over or round – and invariably brings down some soot, however frequently I sweep the chimney, which I do on an average twice a year. And a little soot goes a long way. The spiders contribute much to the dirtying process by making cobwebs in all the many corners, crevices and awkward-to-get-at places. I used to think, as do most people, that spiders spun webs to catch flies. Now I'm not so sure. All that our spiders seem to catch is dust. There are no flies for the greater part of the year. What the spiders live on is a mystery to me – other spiders, I suspect. Certain it is that they get fewer and fewer, and those few get bigger and bigger. They live mainly in the dark "bogey-hole" above the bathroom; and if they just stayed there no one would take any notice of them. But they commit suicide by coming down to play in the bath, from which the only exit for them is via the plug-hole, accompanied by a stream of hot water; for neither I nor anyone else will even consider trying to pick them up by hand.

The only other snag is lack of space, a feature which must always have existed, and which in the past must have presented a far more acute problem than it does now. This inconvenience was greatly diminished by the addition of the new kitchen in 1960. Once it had been built, it soon became impossible to imagine how one had managed without it, how the Campions, Rayners and Isons had managed without it for all those years. They, of course, did not have cooker, refrigerator, sink-unit, food-cupboards etc. to house. Neither did they have book-cases, radio, settee, coffee-tables and other necessities of civilised living. But then, we for our part do not have to give house-room to sacks of corn, bales of wool, sides of bacon, cheeses, brewing-tubs, large pots and pans etc. The Isons actually stored their coal inside the house; it was shovelled in through the front door! Lack of bedroom space is the worst part of this restriction – lack of space and lack of accessibility.

There are only two bedrooms, and no possibility whatever of adding to that number. Neither can they be enlarged, nor any more furniture or cupboard-space be contrived. Access to the bedrooms is now what it was 300 years ago – extremely awkward. Large items such as wardrobe and chest of drawers could only be got into the bedroom by dismantling, passing up through the space between two rafters, where a removable floor-board was left for the purpose, and re-assembling inside the bedroom. On the occasions, fortunately rare, when someone has had to be brought down the stairs on a stretcher, the stretcher-bearers have performed a feat surpassing even their habitual miracles.

The rest is all gain. From the purely physical aspect, living in a thatched cottage is sheer joy. In the depth of winter, when bitter winds howl down the village-street, "straight from the Urals" as they say, or when frost and snow make even a short journey a misery, one can draw up the arm-chair closer to a blazing log-fire and let the elements do their worst. What if 70% of the heat does go up the chimney? The other 30% is mighty comfortable to the feet and legs, and very satisfying to the mind. When the fire is not on duty – and equally when it is – the electric storage-heaters are there in the background. Here we score heavily over the Campions and the Rayners. They had no radiators – they just went to bed. We can truly say that we do not feel the cold, especially since we eliminated draughts by building a greenhouse at the back door and having the front door – which we never used anyway – bricked up. Nor, in summer, do we notice the heat, until we go outside. The insulating property of that thatch is even more effective against heat than against cold.

But the greatest boon of all, from both the physical and mental point of view, is the silence. For whole days and nights, weeks even, one does not seem to hear anything – anything, that is, which compels attention – except the song of birds. Cars and buses pass along the street, aeroplanes fly overhead; but at most they make a gentle subdued sound which has ceased before one is fully conscious of it. Visitors sometimes find this silence disconcerting, especially town-dwellers. We nearly always return from town with a slight headache or a feeling of irritation which vanishes within minutes, almost, once inside the house. The Campions and Rayners must have known this silence, and for them it must have constituted an important element in their feeling of security. So long as all was quiet, all was well; the prowling marauder, the ailing beast, the fidgety dog would have been soon noticed. They, like us, would have had to go outside to know what the weather was like; particularly to find out whether it was raining – this often causes momentary panic on washing-day, just as it must have done in the time of Hannah Campion or Sarah Rayner.

Not a little of the quality of the cottage is due, of course, to its situation, which is almost unique; quite unique in that it was, until recent times, the only house in the village facing east. It has been said that the original orientation of houses was determined by the desire to avoid the direct assault of plague-bearing winds, when for centuries it was thought that the plague must be air-borne. I do not believe that there is any truth in this assertion. Houses in villages, in the vast majority of cases, faced the street; houses in towns, and some in villages where space was limited, were built end-on to the street; and houses everywhere turned their back or their shoulder on their neighbours if they could. What really determined the orientation of a house, then as now, was the site itself. And there can be very few sites in the whole country to surpass the site of this house.

Another aspect of siting was one which, originally, had real practical significance, and which nowadays is of great esthetic value, namely having the countryside "at the back door". Look at the old houses in any village which is still a village and not a glorified town-suburb – you will find that from every house it is possible to go out of the back door (back door, mind you, not the front!) hop over the garden fence or through a gap or gate left in it, and be in open country right away. The practical importance of this feature for centuries was that it enabled one to get to and from one's work with greater ease. It partly explains the utter indifference with which village people regarded the appalling state of the roads in medieval and more recent times, and the fact that for them the roads were not so much highways as places in which they dumped their rubbish or from which they dug the material for building their houses. Look at the Enclosure Map of any village, and see how many footpaths were "stopped up"; there were seventeen in this village, nearly forty in Thriplow; they were all, without exception, at the back of the houses. There was the further advantage that one could leave the house and return to it without being seen, no inconsiderable advantage if one were carrying a couple of rabbits, or a pheasant, or some such burden better not displayed to all and sundry!

This cottage has, I'm glad to say, retained such a situation. The open country is still so near that its natural inhabitants, ignoring such boundaries as there are, do not have to be sought or fetched. In the early days of our occupation, when there was an overgrown orchard next door and an equally overgrown farm-yard just over the bottom fence, it was a common thing to have rabbits running about the lawn and nibbling the carnations, a pair of partridges having a dust-bath in the seed-bed, or pheasants – as many as four all together one frosty morning – scratching for worms. On one memorable occasion a woodcock, needing a breather after his long flight straight from Norway, chose the garden as a temporary home and lived on the remains of an over-fed dog's dinner for a couple of days. Without leaving the house, one could see the hares lolloping about on West Hill, and a light covering of snow revealed the fact that they frequently invaded the garden. Since the new farm-house was built, and the orchard replaced by a pair of houses, the countryside has not been quite so near, and it is rare nowadays to see any livestock actually in the garden, other than pigeons and sparrows, of which I see too many for my liking. We still get more than our fair share of pleasant birds, however. Every year a pair of goldfinches nests in one of the apple-trees; blackbirds, thrushes, linnets, finches, tits abound; and, of course, the inevitable robin or two – the latter tame enough to invade the kitchen when the door is left open, and even, just once, to feed from the hand. The only regular animal visitor now is a grey squirrel. He, or they – I don't know how many there are – is often to be seen perched on the roof-ridge, in the lee of the chimney if a chill wind is blowing. Every autumn he raids a nearby walnut-tree and hides the nuts in the garden. I have watched him rediscover them in the spring, behaving in such a way that it was obvious that he knew where many of them were, but also forgetting just as many. Later in the year I have had to uproot as many as forty little walnut-trees, for he never plants them where I want them.

Speaking of the garden, that, of course, is one of our greatest assets, even though I have reached the stage of life at which it is more enjoyable to sit in a garden than to work in it. The trouble with gardens, when you are getting on in years, is that they are too much at ground level; they involve too much bending, however mechanised your equipment may be. Still, it is well worth having, for the pleasure of being able to taste really new potatoes, really ripe tomatoes, fresh runner beans, young carrots etc., and to enjoy the sight and smell of masses of roses, dahlias, chrysanthemums and scores of other flowers whose names I don't even try to remember. I have tried many times to determine which part or parts of the garden have been used as such for the past five hundred years, and have reached the conclusion that, for much of that time, there was very little area under cultivation. Most of what is now garden was occupied by the yard, sheds, barn and stables. I have dug out the remains of posts, and removed tons of gravel. The garden of the Campions and Rayners seems to have been limited to an area immediately round the house, in which they would have grown onions, radishes, herbs — perhaps as many as a dozen different herbs — but very few flowers.

My thoughts come naturally back to the Campions and the Rayners, to the Isons and the Peppercorns, at every turn. It is not possible to forget them. Not because they "haunt" the place. I don't believe in such nonsense as haunting. But I do believe that, once you *know* the past history of a place, and can *see* part of the past, then that past becomes alive and part of the present. Will Peppercorn and Samuel Campion are as much a part of this house as I am. That is what gives the place an "atmosphere" — for want of a better word — and to live in that atmosphere is to live a life which in some strange way is enriched. Do not, I beg you, accuse me of "living in the past", or of indulging in nostalgic nonsense. Much as I deplore many modern tendencies and values, I live in the present because I am in the present. I do not wish to put the clock back and restore the past — but there's no harm done in taking a look at it. Is there?

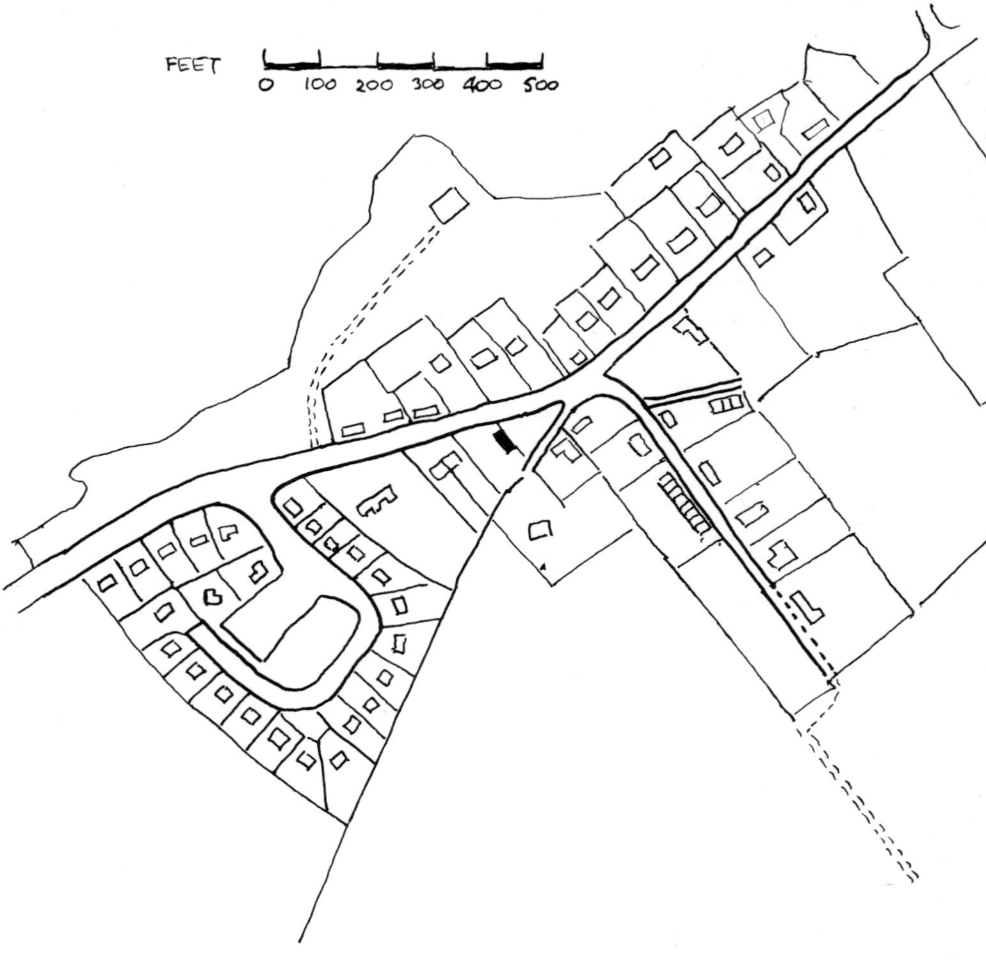

Fig. 18 The West End of Foxton today. Fifty of the houses on this map have been built in the last ten years. The open country is still "at the back door".

EPILOGUE

And there my story ends. But not, I like to think, the history of this house. It will not last for ever, of course. Even those oak beams will one day rot and crumble away, however clever may be the scientists at finding new preservatives. Barring accidents such as fire, however, I feel confident of another three or four hundred years for the life of the frame of the cottage. The roof is a totally different matter. When it was last thatched, there were still binders, sheaves, straight unbroken straw. There are none now. The straw spewed out by the combine-harvester is virtually useless – dirty, twisted, broken; it looks reasonable for a few months, but it just cannot be laid as a real thatch should be laid. There is the possibility of reed – at a price – but the supply of reed is by no means guaranteed. Plastic "straw", perhaps? Much as the idea offends my sense of propriety, I would welcome it if it meant another few hundred years of life. For the cottage, that is, not for me. No amount of plastic wonders will lengthen my allotted span. I shall go, and whoever follows me will go. With any luck, the cottage will go on, and some day, maybe, another scribe will take up the story. A story beginning with "One Parker, a yeoman writer."